Cuban Theater in the United States:

A Critical Anthology

Bilingual Press/Editorial Bilingüe

Address:
Bilingual Review/Press
Hispanic Research Center
Arizona State University
Tempe, Arizona 85287
(602) 965-3867

DATE DUE

12. 20.			
04. 01. 95			
JUL 29 2004			

28-2

Cuban Theater in the United States:

A Critical Anthology

Luis F. González-Cruz

Francesca M. Colecchia

editors and translators

Bilingual Press/Editorial Bilingüe

TEMPE, ARIZONA

All inquiries regarding performance rights to these plays should be addressed to the publisher: Bilingual Press, Hispanic Research Center, Arizona State University, Tempe, Arizona, 85287-2702. (602) 965-3867

ISBN 0-927534-26-6 (cloth)
ISBN 0-927534-27-4 (paper)

Library of Congress Cataloging-in-Publication Data

Cuban theater in the United States : a critical anthology / edited and translated by Luis F. González-Cruz and Francesca M. Colecchia.
p. cm.
Translated from the Spanish.
Includes bibliographical references (p.).
ISBN 0-927534-26-6 (cloth). — ISBN 0-927534-27-4 (paper)
1. American drama—Cuban American authors. 2. Cuban American drama (Spanish)—Translations into English. 3. Cuban Americans—Drama. I. González-Cruz, Luis F., 1943- II. Colecchia, Francesca.
PS628.C82C834 1992
862—dc20 92-308
CIP

PRINTED IN THE UNITED STATES OF AMERICA

Cover design by Kerry Curtis

Acknowledgments

The editors would like to express their appreciation to the playwrights for permission to publish their works and to translate them into English where necessary.

This volume is supported by a grant from the National Endowment for the Arts in Washington, D.C., a Federal agency.

Contents

To our mothers

Introduction

Today there are at least forty-five recognized Cuban playwrights residing in the United States. Their plays have received literary awards and been staged, radio broadcasted, published, and publicly read. This great number of dramatists seems disproportionate to the number of Cuban immigrants who have come to the United States in the last three decades. The phenomenon is the result of an artistic, intellectual, and literary process which evolved on the island since the mid-1930s; and the nature, configuration, and specific circumstances surrounding the Cuban exodus which began after the triumph of the revolution in 1959.

Until the beginning of the nineteenth century, a truly autochthonous theater had not existed in Cuba. The productions up to then had reflected, with some delay, the styles and modes of the existing Spanish theater. By the middle of the century, Gertrudis Gómez de Avellaneda (1814-1873), a Cuban poet and playwright residing in Spain, had written three important dramas in the romantic vein: *Munio Alfonso, Saúl,* and *Baltasar,* as well as comedies, including *La hija de las flores.* At the same time in Cuba the poets Joaquín Lorenzo Luaces (1821-1867) and José Jacinto Milanés (1814-1863) also authored plays of considerable quality. During the same period, another kind of theater known as *teatro bufo* (*bufo:* comic), with roots reaching deep into the heart of the Cuban soul, emerged. It utilized Cuban slang, stock folk characters, and popular music. This was a humorous, light theatrical genre, rich in *choteo,*[1] which frequently degenerated into the gross or plainly vulgar.

Independence from Spain, achieved in 1898 at the end of the Cuban wars of independence, gave Cuban writers new opportunities and stimulated in them the desire to assert their nationhood. Naturally, the theater reflected this new attitude.

The first noticeable impact of Cuban independence on the theater was the lack of restraint in *teatro bufo* which moved from an occasional vulgarity to the bluntly pornographic. On the other hand, forthright plays dealing with national identity were written in the first two decades of the twentieth century, slowly preparing the way for the explosion in theater which would occur in the late 1930s. The popular Alhambra Theater, home of Havana's *teatro bufo* for so many years was demolished in 1935, a symbolic event which held the promise of a more auspicious future for Cuban theater. Theater people and playwrights, who until then had depended almost entirely on what traditional Spanish repertory companies brought to the island, gradually opened their eyes to the new theatrical movements in Europe and the United States. The outcome of this formidable and transforming process was the birth of numerous theatrical groups in the years to follow: Grupo La Cueva (1936), Teatro Cubano de Selección (1938), ADADEL (1940), Teatro Universitario (1941), Patronato del Teatro (1942), Teatro Popular (1943), Theatralia (1943), ADAD (1945), Academia Municipal de Artes Dramáticas (1947), Prometeo (1947), Farseros (1947), Compañía Dramática Cubana (1947), Grupo Escénico Libre (1949), Las Máscaras (1950), Arena (1953), and Teatro Estudio (1955). Many of these groups did not perform year-round, nor did they have a fixed site or theater on which to stage their productions.

The influence of the major figures of the contemporary stage—Stanislavski, Appia, Copeau, Craig, Reinhardt, Meyerhold, Piscator, and Brecht—was strongly felt at one point or another by the creators of Cuban theater. Many Cuban playwrights received training in the officially established schools such as the Seminario de Arte Dramático de la Universidad de la Habana and the already mentioned Academia Municipal de Artes Dramáticas, while others went to perfect their craft abroad. Playwrights would acquaint themselves with the wealth of world drama not only through their readings, but also through performances of plays from the Greeks through Ionesco. By the mid-1950s, theatrical activity had reached such a peak in Cuba that theaters sprung up in Havana at a considerable speed given the population of the Cuban capital. An evergrowing, enthusiastic theater-going audience developed. Among the most active theaters doing serious work at the time were TEDA, Arcoiris, Arlequín, Atelier, El Sótano, Hubert de Blanck, Las Máscaras, Los Comediantes, Prometeo, and Talía. This was, of course, in addition to the larger theaters which presented a variety of popular shows, *zarzuelas* (Spanish or Cuban musicals), and occasional foreign performing groups which continued to visit the country.

Among the Cuban playwrights whose works were performed

during this period, some names, spanning two generations, are worth noting: Luis A. Baralt, Carlos Felipe, Virgilio Piñera (whose play *Falsa alarma* is considered the first example of theater of the absurd in Latin America), Eduardo Manet (who lives in France and writes mainly in French), Matías Montes Huidobro, and Antón Arrufat. The names of others who established their reputation after 1959, like those of José Triana (now residing in France and author of the internationally successful *La noche de los asesinos*), Abelardo Estorino, and Nicolás Dorr, should be added to the list.

The advent of the revolution in 1959 brought about profound changes in Cuban society, the most significant being the exodus of the middle and professional classes followed by a good portion of the working class. This emigration took place at a very rapid pace during the 1960s, slowed down somewhat during the 1970s, and peaked in 1980 with the boatlift from the port of Mariel which transported over 100,000 refugees to the United States. Cuban exiles settled all over the country, but the major concentrations are in the New York/New Jersey areas and in Miami, where the Cuban community is the larger and more prosperous of the two groups.

Although some important performing artists left Cuba at the very beginning of the revolutionary period, it was not until the mid-1960s that writers and artists in different fields, including theater professionals, started to leave in greater numbers. The reasons for this expatriation lie in the ideological demands of the revolutionary government—which grew more severe after Castro's famous address, "Palabras a los intelectuales," in 1961—and in the moralistic repression, systematically enforced beginning in 1965, which constrained so many creative people. Because of this migration, a theater movement developed within the Cuban population of both Miami and New York.

A survey of the plays by Cuban exiles reveals a few decisive attributes in common. All of these playwrights have a historical awareness as if all wished, or felt obligated, to leave a written account of their unique experience. At the same time, they consider not only the possible impact or the recognition their plays could have in the present, but also the place that the future will assign to them and their works. They are conscious of the roles they are playing as witnesses, spokespersons, and prophets in a historical drama that has profoundly shaken their country of origin and ultimately made exiles of many of its people.

It is our contention that exile, whether voluntary or involuntary, has been a major factor behind these writers' creativity and has affected the nature of their work. In general, writers find in exile an adequate milieu in which to work because writers are by nature exiles who view the world from their own individual and, therefore, unique perspective. They are at the same time distanced from and paradoxically involved with the reality about which they write. True exile, geographic exile, forces people to settle in a land not their own and at the same time heightens their awareness of their own identity, causes to appraise and scrutinize their circumstances, and to ponder what they left behind and what now sustains them. It also involves an unavoidable process of adaptation to what can be termed foreign living conditions. This is the one element that greatly differentiates one Cuban exile playwright from another. The degree of adaptation to the new land depends to a great extent on the length of time the person has lived in the "new country" and the age at which the person left the "old one." One must keep in mind that the Cuban migration has taken place during a period of some thirty years.

In this anthology, next to playwrights who left Cuba at the beginning of the revolution (Matías Montes Huidobro and Leopoldo Hernández), the reader will find others who left at a very young age and have developed their creative talents in the United States (Héctor Pérez and Manuel Pereiras). The older generation normally writes in Spanish; the younger uses either Spanish or English. Those who came during the Mariel exodus, educated and intellectually formed in Cuba—some of whom, like Reinaldo Arenas and René Ariza, served prison terms for their dissidence—have preferred Spanish as their literary language. While the older generation opposes Castro, the youngest writers show a less intense political radicalism. There are even some cases of open admiration of the Castro regime, especially among those who left Cuba soon after 1959.

Our anthology represents a selection made from 150 plays. All the writers included here left Cuba after the advent of Castro. The plays are short and deal with a variety of themes. The topics of *machismo* and Afro-Cuban religion appear in Matías Montes Huidobro's play, *Olofe's Razor.* In Julio Matas's work, *Dialogue of the Poet and the Supreme Leader,* the main character, a paradigm of "the man who thinks," is a poet who finds himself trapped in a political dilemma. Leopoldo Hernández, in his play *We Were Always Afraid,* confronts two different realities, that of a Cuban woman who has chosen to remain on the island under Castro, and that of her brother, an exile who has lived many years in Los Angeles and who has returned for one of the short family visits allowed by the Cuban government beginning in 1979. Although René Ariza presents a stylized view of revolutionary Cuba in *The Meeting,* the rest of his mini-dramas included here *(Doll's Play, Declaration of Principles,* and *A Flower Vendor for These Times)* deal with psychological questions of a universal nature. In Reinaldo Arenas's play, *Traitor,* the audience observes a Utopian moment in history when Castro's regime has fallen, and justice, or as he suggests, *the injustice of justice,* triumphs amid chaos. Miguel González-Pando also sets his work, *The Great American Justice Game,* in the future, a future in which Spanish/English bilingualism is illegal. The vision of the future becomes apocalyptic in Dolores Prida's play, *Screens,* which confronts the audience with the reality of a world in the aftermath of a nuclear disaster. Of all the works offered here, the most universal in their themes are, perhaps, those of Héctor Pérez and Manuel Pereiras. In Pérez's play, *Perhaps the Marshland,* the young "Bumboy," who at the end will venture into the marshland, symbolizes the possible birth of something better. In Pereiras's drama, *The Marriage of Hippolyta,* a poetic aura envelops the intriguing dialogue taking the audience through bold passionate conflicts, ending in an inevitable catastrophe.

In our selection process we have taken into account first, the quality of the plays, and then the established reputation of some of the writers, the potential found in other less known dramatists, and especially the staging possibilities of all the works. As a result, some important playwrights whose one-act plays did not conform to our purposes or repeated themes present in plays already selected were not included. Other prestigious playwrights have written only full-length plays which exceed the scope of this collection.

The present anthology combines theater pieces that are representative of the varied theatrical trends and styles of the different generations of Cuban dramatists living[2] in the United States. The number of research articles and critical works, whose reference we have incorporated in the bibliography, testifies to the considerable effort and reputation of these Cuban writers who have become a part of American culture, and who represent an important and distinct voice among the growing Hispanic communities. If, in their present form, these plays find their way to the stages of academic and professional theatrical groups and thus reach English-speaking audiences, we will have achieved our goals.

Luis F. González-Cruz
Francesca Colecchia

Notes

[1]A colloquial term used in Cuba to describe an attitude of disrespect which is linguistically manifested by chaffing or jeering.

[2]Reinaldo Arenas passed away after the selection of plays to be included in this anthology had been made.

A Partial List of Cuban Dramatists Residing in the United States

Acevedo, Nena (Children's plays)
Acosta, Iván
Alomá, René (Died in 1986)
Arenas, Reinaldo (Died in 1990)
Ariza, René
Barceló, Randy
Blanco, Rafael
Borges, Fermín (Died in 1987)
Caturla de la Maza, Olga (Children's plays)
Cid Pérez, José
Clavijo, Uva
Corrales, José
De Cárdenas, Raúl
Fornés, María Irene
García, Patti Allen
González, Alberto
González, Celedonio
González Esteva, Orlando
González-Pando, Miguel
Guigou, Alberto
Hernández, Leopoldo
Machado, Eduardo
Martín, Manuel
Martín, Mario
Matas, Julio
Montes Huidobro, Matías
Nóbregas, Andrés
O'Farrill, Julio
Ortal, Yolanda
Peña, Mario
Pereiras, Manuel
Pérez, Héctor
Prida, Dolores
Quiroga, José
Rodríguez Sardiñas, Orlando
Romaguera, Luis

Romaguera, Luis (Jr.)
Román, Pedro
Sánchez-Boudy, José
Santeiro, Luis
Simo, Ana María
Taillacq, Evelio
Torres, Omar
Travieso, Tomás
Valls, Jorge
Vieira, Juan

We Were Always Afraid

Leopoldo Hernández

Leopoldo Hernández

Born in Havana in 1921, Leopoldo Hernández has written more than fifty plays, many of which have been staged successfully in Cuba (before 1961) and in the United States. In Cuba he won several prizes for his plays, including *La pendiente* (1959), *El barquito de papel* (1961), and *El mudo* (1961). The latter, as well as his *Los huesos*, were staged in Cuba in 1961. Numerous productions followed in the United States: *Guáimaro* (1969), *940 South West Segunda Calle* (1969), *Liberación* (1969), *Hollywood 70* (1970), *Ana* (1971), *Hollywood 73* (1973), *Martínez* (1981), *Do Not Negotiate Mr. President* (1983), *We Were Always Afraid* (1987), as well as others. In 1986 Hernández was named a finalist for his play, *Tres azules para Michael*, in the prestigious contest, "Premios Literarios Letras de Oro," sponsored by the American Express Company and the University of Miami.

His published plays include *La espalda, La consagración del miedo,* and *Los hombres mueren solos* (in *Teatro de la Revolución*, Mexico, 1958 [under the pseudonym Karlo Tomas]); *La pendiente* (Havana: Imprenta Ponciano, 1959); *Sombras* (in *Diario Libre*, Havana, October 25, 1959); and *Mañana el sol* (in *Revista Mester*, Los Angeles, 1973). Hernández has also written many short stories published in Cuba, the United States, and Spain.

Leopoldo Hernández received a doctorate in 1945 from the School of Law of the University of Havana. He worked as a radio announcer and producer for station CMCB in Havana in the 1940s, and later in the legal departments of several major companies in that city. He and his wife, Josefina, left Cuba for Miami, settling there on November 1, 1961. Three years later they moved to Los Angeles, where they lived for twenty years while he worked as a lease analyst for Union Oil Company of California. During those years he also wrote extensively. Upon his retirement in 1984 they returned to

Miami. In rather poor health for a number of years, Hernández, aided by Josefina, continues to participate in major theatrical events in the Miami area.

The version of *We Were Always Afraid* included here is based on an adaptation by Rafael de Acha of the original longer play, which we have further revised, trying to remain faithful to both the style and spirit of the Spanish original. The drama takes place after 1979 when the Cuban government began allowing Cuban exiles to return for family visits. Hernández brings together a brother and sister separated for some twenty years. He, residing in Los Angeles, returns to the family home in Cuba where she has remained, suffering the social, political, and economic pressures of Castroism. As the man goes back to the home he had abandoned, he comes to realize that time and circumstances have altered everything. Out of the need to survive, even his sister has changed. Hernández suggests that both are guilty of their destiny as well as victims of it. His reality abroad and hers on the island are presented as antithetical and irreconcilable. For the characters, life continues along its course. When they look back at their mistakes, they realize it is too late to remedy anything: they must suffer the consequences of their errors. The hereditary illness that has begun to affect brother and sister serves as an omen of the inevitable end that awaits them—alone and separated from one another—in the sad place each has chosen to live.

We Were Always Afraid

Characters

HE, a man in his late fifties who looks younger than his age.
SHE, a woman in her early sixties who looks older. Shakes from time to time as a result of early Parkinson's disease.

Setting

The living room of a middle-class family in Havana. Pictures on the walls. An old record player placed not far from an equally old television set. Furniture is dated and worn. Two rocking chairs at stage center in which the actors sit.

SHE: They'll be here soon. They probably went down to the beach. It's nearby. You remember, don't you?
HE: Even after twenty years? Sure. It's three blocks that way.
SHE: It's nice to go there and breathe the fresh sea air. Good for the lungs.
HE: How are our aunts?
SHE: Didn't I write you that they passed away?
HE: I guess you did . . . I'm sorry.
SHE: With so many relatives gone, it must be hard for you to keep track of who's dead and who isn't.
HE: I'm sorry.
SHE: It's alright. *(Long awkward pause.)* Well, there are so many things to talk about . . . Do you . . . like where you're living in Los Angeles?
HE: It's a city like any other city. Only it's big, very big. In fact, enormous. Every once in a while, it trembles.

SHE: You don't say! . . . And are there lots of people there?

HE: Millions and millions.

SHE: It must be nice.

HE: Wonderful. You can't go out at night or you get mugged. And there are the blacks who hate the Mexicans, who hate the Koreans, who hate the Jews, who hate them all. Not really a very pleasant place.

SHE: And I thought you were happy . . .

HE: At least I'm free. It's nice to live in a country where freedom's guaranteed by the government and the law.

SHE: *(Changing the subject.)* I understand all the movie stars live there.

HE: *(Not hearing her.)* When's the family coming?

SHE: I already told you.

HE: My entry permit's good for two days, that's all . . . God knows I don't want to stay here any more than I have to.

SHE: They'll be here any moment now.

HE: If I don't get to see them today, I'm going back home tomorrow anyway . . . After all, I'll have seen you.

SHE: I beg you not to talk like that . . . They'll be here soon.

HE: Tell me the truth, please.

SHE: I told you!

HE: The truth.

SHE: They're scared . . . they're afraid . . .

HE: *(Emphatically.)* Of me?

SHE: Of what you might say or do. They remember you. We used to talk about you all the time.

HE: *Used* to?

SHE: I . . . mean . . . *(She cannot complete her sentence.)*

HE: Words fail you, but your silence speaks louder than words.

SHE: Please, let's stop hurting each other.

HE: You're right. No one's really to blame. *(Long pause.)* How's your granddaughter?

SHE: Wonderful. Her school grades couldn't be better. And she's a soloist with the school chorus. Last week she sang in a concert. Her solo was the Inter . . . *(She stops cold.)* The . . . Anthem.

HE: They get them when they're little, don't they? The little red youth pioneer sings the Internationale in place of our national anthem. That's just great!

SHE: Please change the subject.

HE: As you wish.

SHE: *(Another long awkward pause.)* I guess you visit your friends who live in Los Angeles.

HE: Not too often. The distances are enormous.

SHE: What about your cousin?

HE: He moved to New York. He came to see me once . . . or maybe he was in town on business and decided to say hello. Once a year I get a Christmas card from him. I guess he's a homosexual.

SHE: How could you say such a horrible thing?

HE: What's so horrible about that?

SHE: He's a good man!

HE: I didn't say he was *bad*, only that I thought he was a homosexual. In fact in New York it's considered a good thing to be one. Very convenient. Down here either you're macho or a fag. Nothing in between. Probably that's why so many left. Had he stayed here, he would have wound up in one of the internment camps.

SHE: Let's talk about something else. God in heaven, you haven't changed. Still the same opinionated, willful person.

HE: That's why father hated me.

SHE: But mother worshipped you. And father didn't hate you. He never hated anyone.

HE: Let's say that my behavior scared him.

SHE: With you getting into all kinds of trouble, he had good reason.

HE: Trouble?

SHE: Yes, trouble: protests, strikes, fights, that sort of stuff.

HE: Like a real leader of the people.

SHE: More like a stubborn idiot.

HE: Thanks.

SHE: You're welcome! *(Pause.)* They were good parents and they loved you the best.

HE: Typical Latins, the son was the center of the universe.

SHE: And women were for sewing and singing: coser y cantar!

HE: You wouldn't want to be a lawyer . . . and a . . . *frustrated* writer.

SHE: You wouldn't want to be a housewife . . . and a . . . *frustrated* musician.

HE: *(Noticing her trembling hands.)* Mom had it too. Now it's our turn.

SHE: You too?

HE: Sure. The early stages, but it's there alright.

SHE: I didn't know that.

HE: Why should I bother you with my troubles?

SHE: But your hand doesn't shake . . .

HE: Once in a while. Truth is I already have trouble with soup spoons. *(Pause.)* We'll both end up slobbering like babies. Shuffling. Finally bedridden and incontinent. Not a pleasant outlook.

SHE: But mother never got that bad.

HE: She was the lucky one. She died of cancer at fifty.

SHE: Lucky? Lucky? God! How can you . . .

HE: *(Interrupting her.)* Just a figure of speech. Let's talk about some of my old schoolmates.

SHE: Why? They're all gone—dead or in prison.

HE: Rolando got out through the French embassy. He lives in Paris now.

SHE: What about Raimundo?

HE: Blew out his brains in Miami . . . *Is* there life after Miami?

SHE: Brother, we haven't seen each other in twenty years. We were younger then. When you leave today, or tomorrow, we'll probably *never* see each other again. Can we *please* take advantage of these few precious hours and talk about more pleasant things?

HE: Alright, you talk.

SHE: *(Searching for something to say.)* Well . . . for instance . . . Commander Trejo made us a gift of . . .

HE: *(Interrupting her violently.)* That bastard son of a whore gave you what? A copy of the dossier he took to the police when I was barely twenty. The man who nearly had me castrated with an electric prod—like they use for cattle—for "subversive activities contrary to the stability and welfare of the Republic." That one? That turncoat, professional squealer—now a commander? That professional quisling and executioner! First with one regime, then with another, then—maybe someday—into exile in Miami to publish an anti-something or other piece of yellow journalism, or to do a radio show for the exile community that he and others like him put into exile. Oh my God, but you are naive. You? I ought to say *all of us*—a naive, incestuous bunch of third-world retrogrades!!! Trejo indeed! Next he'll be marrying my niece.

SHE: He gave us something we needed very much. And we didn't know . . .

HE: Which I don't care to know about! God! *Now* I understand what it is that makes that family of yours—this family of *mine*—tick.

Here, in a country where your next-door neighbor knows your every coming and going, where you can't have a barbecue in your backyard without having the head of the surveillance committee come around snooping, inspecting, reporting . . . here you didn't know who Trejo is, or was? Come now!

SHE: I swear, I didn't . . .

HE: *You didn't know?*

SHE: No. We didn't.

HE: Look, it's better if I leave. It's not worth it! I'm making you suffer. You're making me regret the day I ever thought of coming back. Good-bye!

SHE: Stay! . . . Please! . . . Stay.

HE: What for?

SHE: For our parents.

HE: They neither see, nor hear, nor think, nor feel. They're in that eternal vacuum in which there are no shapes, no messages, no feelings, no betrayals, no pain. They both died over twenty years ago, within a month of each other. I got two telegrams. And all I had left were two memories and a piece of yellow paper. When I broke up with my wife I died a little too. We used to argue, just the way our parents used to argue. God, how I loved her! And now I live alone, with my work, my books, my writing.

SHE: Why don't you marry again?

HE: I'd better go.

SHE: You can stay here if you wish. But I already know your answer.

HE: I'm glad you're that perceptive.

SHE: I feel sorry for you.

HE: Don't be. I'm a survivor.

SHE: You're a hardened man.

HE: I graduated from the School of Hard Knocks, cum laude.

SHE: I don't follow you.

HE: Two exiles, two revolutions, two failures, a broken marriage. Life continues: I hang on, I work, I write, I keep on going.

SHE: And here you are.

HE: And here I *was.* I'm leaving!

SHE: They'll be here soon.

HE: I doubt it.

SHE: You haven't said one word about your impressions of our town after twenty years.

HE: What do you want me to say? I don't want to hurt you any more.

SHE: Come on. Tell me.

HE: A sad city. No traffic in the streets, no vendors of those snacks I used to love as a child. No soul! Only advisors: Bulgarians, Hungarians, Russians, North Koreans. They all smell the same. The worst dressed, worst smelling people in the world.

SHE: Our next door neighbors are Czechs. Lovely family. She's a teacher of Slavic Languages at the Institute; he's an engineer.

HE: I bet they don't have to line up to buy soap.

SHE: *(Attempting a joke.)* Who says they use it? They give us their soap. After they leave the house, their body odor lingers on for hours and hours.

HE: But they don't have to stand in line.

SHE: What matters is that *they* bring me all I need from the special store for foreigners, and charge me only what they spend.

HE: What matters is that those items are for sale to Czechs, Bulgarians, Italian diplomats, Chinese interpreters, and German tourists, but not to you and your family. And when your Eastern European charity comes knocking at the door, all you do is be grateful. The irony of it all never hits you.

SHE: Survival. That's the only thing that matters. I thank God every day for our Czech charity.

HE: I'm really not interested in spending my last few minutes with you discussing how nice your neighbors are. Let me use the phone.

SHE: Of course. I can tell you one thing though. If you're planning to call Bravo, you're in for a big surprise.

HE: What do you mean?

SHE: Call him.

HE: What do you mean?

SHE: Just call him.

HE: Alright! I will! *(Goes to the telephone and dials.)* . . . Hello . . . Is this señora Bravo? This is your husband's friend from Los Angeles . . . I'm sure he's mentioned me to you . . . Oh? . . . Is he in? . . . Why? . . . He isn't sick, is he? . . . Then why can't he . . . Look señora Bravo, I'm only here until tomorrow . . . But . . . Please tell him that I'm at my sister's, and that I'd like to speak to him before I leave . . . Will you please do that?- . . . Thank you . . . Good-bye! *(He hangs up.)*

SHE: He won't call you.

HE: Yes he will! He's like a brother to me.

SHE: He won't call you. He's not sick. He's not at work, not on a Sunday. He just isn't going to pick up that phone.

HE: *(Pause.)* Are you trying to tell me he's playing the same game my brother-in-law and the rest of the family are playing?

SHE: It's no game, dear brother, just caution.

HE: Bravo's not a coward. He'll call me!

SHE: He won't call you. He's a writer, like you. They watch them constantly.

HE: The Inquisition.

SHE: The system.

HE: Damn the system! I know he'll call me!

SHE: He won't. He wouldn't survive if he did.

HE: I can't believe this is happening. They've changed you. They've changed your world! They've taken everything away and just left you a pile of slogans, some memories, and the damned fear.

SHE: It's not perfect, but it's all we have to live with.

HE: Love it or leave it?

SHE: Love it or leave it.

HE: *(Very long pause.)* I still think he'll call me.

SHE: If I were you, I wouldn't hold my breath.

HE: I haven't held my breath waiting for that family of yours to come.

SHE: Maybe they don't realize you're here already.

HE: They won't come.

SHE: There could be any number of reasons . . . Maybe they went for ice cream . . .

HE: They won't come.

SHE: Why do you go on like this? Can we try somehow to catch up on twenty lost years?

HE: How can we begin to? Here I stand, a total stranger, a pariah. They don't want to see me . . . Bravo won't come to the phone.

The telephone rings.

HE: *(Excited.)* I bet it's Bravo.

SHE: *(Picking up the telephone.)* Hello.

HE: *(Stretching out his hand.)* Give me the phone.

SHE: *(Shaking her head and placing a finger on her lips to indicate silence.)* Yes, comrade. How are your? *(Pause.)* My brother *(Pause.)* . . . Yes, he arrived . . . *(Pause.)* No, the rest of the family hasn't seen him.

They left early this morning. *(Pause.)* Yes, he knows about that. *(Pause.)* Tomorrow, of course. *(Hangs up.)*

HE: Somebody from the committee, right?

SHE: Right. She . . .

HE: What'd she want to know?

SHE: She wanted to know if the others had seen you and . . .

HE: . . . and to make sure I'd be leaving tomorrow?

SHE: Yes.

HE: *(Defiant.)* Give me the phone. I'm gonna try Bravo again.

SHE: He won't answer.

HE: *(Dialing.)* We'll see.

SHE: *(Reaching to take the telephone from him.)* But . . .

HE: *(Stopping her with a gesture of the left hand.)* Yes, this is the comrade from the Defense Committee. Tell your husband that I must speak with him at once. *(Pause, as he waves her away with the left hand.)*

HE: Bravo? I bet you know who's speaking. *(Pause.)* What are you saying? *(Pause.)* Don't do that to me, brother. That's what you are, and always have been to me. A brother. Don't fail me like that. *(Pause.)* But . . . *(Pause.)* All I ask is that you listen to me for a minute. In one minute a lot can be said. *(Pause.)* Please, let's talk for just a minute. And don't interrupt me anymore with that "I don't know who you are" bull. You know who I am and that I called earlier . . . *(Pause.)* Look, in spite of politics, I'm still your friend and politics shouldn't keep us apart. *(Pause.)* Do you hear me? . . . Hello. Hello. *(Pause, as he looks at his sister.)* He hung up on me. *(She stretches her arm to take the phone which she puts in its place. There is a heavy, extremely painful silence.)*

SHE: I'm sorry.

HE: I probably deserved it.

SHE: Why don't you wait a little longer?

HE: I don't think it's worth it.

SHE: We're together. Isn't that worth it?

HE: You, Bravo, your family, the people of this wretched, godforsaken land can't talk, dear sister. You've been gagged. You've been brainwashed. Your souls are barren. It's not a matter of wanting or not wanting to. You simply can't talk. You whisper as if . . . *because* the walls have ears and eyes. You've asked me to lower my voice with your eyes and your hands more than once during the last hour or so. You're even afraid of your family, of the children and their reporting you or your husband to the leaders of the Young Pioneers. This is the consecration of fear . . . They won't come. They know about me and they're afraid of my tongue—loose, free, poisoned. Actually, I was looking forward to seeing your husband as well as my niece who was a kid when I left. Now she's a mother and has a baby of her own. I tell you it's absolutely *incredible*. In this country, fear is a permanent state of mind—fear and suspicion, that is. People are so suspicious of things; they begin to suspect suspicion itself. The only thing, the only gnawing, nagging doubt that I still have to grapple with is why in the name of heaven, or hell, don't you and the other several million people in this country of sheep do something to conquer that permanent state of fear and suspicion. You're sheep . . . no, cowards! Cowards!

SHE: You're the coward! You who, abandoning family and friends, sought the comfort of exile and the protection of an American passport. It's ever so easy for you to pontificate and talk about liberty and speaking your mind! WHAT DO YOU KNOW? You don't have to overcome fear. You don't have to conquer *anything*! You have it easy . . . everything on a silver platter. DON'T TELL ME ABOUT DOING THIS OR THAT OR THE OTHER!

HE: *(After a long, painful pause.)* I'd better go. I've seen you. We've talked.

SHE: Life . . . *(She cannot go on.)*

HE: Life has become difficult for us, difficult and bitter to such an extent that I've come to desire death more and more with each passing day. Death is like a friend who hovers around us all—shy at times, her face hidden, never announcing her arrival. She just sort of drops in uninvited, like an unwanted guest. So many have died . . . so many . . . Sometimes I feel guilty for just still being here. I stop. I look at these hands which shake a little more each day, and I think that, instead of using them for writing poems and plays, I could put them to better use to put an end to this senseless, hopeless, meaningless existence . . . What are these hands good for, anyway?

SHE: For writing. To do with them what you've done ever since you were a child. To do what you are destined to do until God decides otherwise. Use them while you can. They are your instruments.

Some day they'll atrophy and tremble so fiercely you won't have the use of them anymore. But for now, you are doomed to face the blank page and feel the pangs of solitude that come with your work. You are a creator, even if your words destroy. Those hands are your punishment and your glory. I have spent the best moments of the last twenty years of my life reading and re-reading every word you wrote before you left us . . . thousands of pages that you left behind. I've learned to know you and understand you . . . your true self . . . your inner self. I'm sure there are many more thousands of words that have sprung from your head and flowed from your hands in all these years of exile. Endless, infinite joy and punishment. It won't be necessary for you to kill yourself. You'll die when you finish writing about the infinite.

HE: Your words are sincere, but they won't help me make it through the long sleepless nights and the agonizingly lonely hours. I can't wait until I finish writing about the infinite to die, dear sister. There's no future in that. My only sanity is knowing there's an end at hand.

SHE: But you don't deserve it.

HE: I don't deserve a reprieve?

SHE: You don't deserve death; no one does.

HE: Who the hell wants to live forever?

SHE: I do.

HE: With those hands in that condition?

SHE: *(Trying to still the tremors in her hands.)* With these hands in this condition.

HE: I don't understand you.

SHE: I understand you perfectly.

HE: In the past, people killed each other; heads rolled; whole armies were gassed. But friends were friends. Families were families. Today, we're no better than animals . . . worse, actually. Pure evil, wickedness, cowardice. What has happened to Bravo . . . to my family . . . *(His voice trails off.)*

SHE: You've plenty of pity for yourself . . . hardly any for others.

HE: I suffer every day because of it. I ask nothing of others I do not ask of myself. Yes . . . I suffer daily and I punish others for not having the courage to exorcise the fear under which they live . . . fear like shards of broken glass.

SHE: Would you like to walk down to the beach with me, for the . . .

HE: For the last time? No, thanks. Wasn't it one of our poets who wrote that "The sea that surrounds us . . ."

SHE: ". . . is the sea that we turn our backs on . . ."

HE: *(Reciting.)* "From across, and over the sea / Comes the unknown and bitter enemy."

SHE: Unknown and bitter, but not an enemy.

HE: I don't want to see that ocean . . . We've suffered enough for one day.

SHE: Is there anything I can do for you?

HE: I don't think so . . . Is there anything I can do for you?

SHE: Don't write to me anymore.

HE: But . . .

SHE: *(Interrupting.)* Please, not anymore.

HE: We've finally seen each other and for the last time.

SHE: We've seen each other's ghost. The real us faded away a long time ago.

HE: Tomorrow I'll be home.

SHE: Today you came home.

HE: This *was* home, sister.

SHE: Do you call home that place where you wallow in misery and loneliness?

HE: I may not be happy there, but I'm certainly not happy here. At least in that place I call "home" I can sit down and write about this trip to hell and publish it and not fear that someone will come to my door in the middle of the night and drag me away.

SHE: Not even your friend death?

HE: Not even her . . . I'm still afraid . . . But my weapons against fear are this *(Points to his head.)* and this *(Points to his heart.)* and these *(Points to his hands.)*. Perhaps I shall conquer fear. God knows I'll try.

SHE: May He have mercy on your soul!

HE: And on yours!

SHE: Is this good-bye, then?

HE: What more is there to say?

SHE: "From across and over the sea
Comes the unknown and bitter enemy.
The sea that surrounds us
Is the sea that we turn our backs on."

HE: Good-bye.

SHE: You will die when you finish writing about the infinite . . . Good-bye.

He starts to exit slowly, stops, turns around, looks at her and, retracing his steps, opens his arms to embrace her. She walks slowly to him. They embrace.

CURTAIN

Dialogue of the Poet and the Supreme Leader

Julio Matas

Julio Matas

Born in Havana in 1931, Julio Matas is an artist in the fullest sense of the word. A 1952 graduate of the Seminario de Arte Dramático of the University of Havana where he trained both as an actor and as a director, Matas also received a doctorate from the School of Law of the same university in 1955. In 1956 he staged successfully, perhaps for the first time in all of Latin America, Eugene Ionesco's *The Bald Soprano*. His book of poetry, *Homenaje*, was published in 1958, followed by another collection of poems, *Retrato de tiempo*, in 1959. When the Cuban Revolution triumphed in January 1959, Matas was a graduate student at Harvard University. Like the main character in the play presented here, he was lured back to his native country. He returned to Cuba in 1960 to devote himself fully to work in the theater after being offered a position as a director in the National Cuban Theater, a position he held for a brief time. For four years he worked as stage director for several organizations as well as for national television: Departamento de Bellas Artes, Casa de las Américas, Teatro Estudio, Teatro Lírico, and Teleteatro. He was also director of the weekly television program of the literary magazine *Lunes de Revolución*. In 1963 Ediciones Erre published his collection of short stories, *Catálogo de imprevistos* and, in 1964, his first full-length play, *La crónica y el suceso*. Matas returned to the United States in 1965. He received a doctorate in Romance Languages from Harvard University five years later. In 1971 he published a collection of short stories, *Erinia* (Miami: Universal). Three full-length plays (*El extravío, La crónica y el suceso*, and *Aquí cruza el ciervo*) were published in the book *Teatro* (Miami: Universal) in 1990. To date, a few of his plays have appeared in English, among them, *Ladies at Play (Juego de damas)*, widely staged in the United States, and *Penelope Inside, Out (El cambio)*. Matas is also a literary critic and has written several books of criticism. He is presently Professor Emeritus of Hispanic Languages and Literatures at the University of Pittsburgh.

Dialogue of the Poet and the Supreme Leader (Diálogo de Poeta y Máximo), written originally in Spanish, is one of Matas's most recent plays. The Poet, at first a true revolutionary, becomes disillusioned with the new regime that has turned the free society he dreamed about into a totalitarian one. When he ends up in jail, the Supreme Leader comes in person to discuss the Poet's predicament with him. The action which the Leader demands from the Poet for his release is unacceptable to the latter. His destiny, in a system as intolerant as the one described here, is annihilation as a writer and as a human being. Matas gives a balanced account of the ideological battle between the Revolutionary Party and the intellectual dissidents. The playwright's intention is not to take sides—although by the simple act of writing this play he does—but to present face-to-face the two archetypal political philosophies which struggle today to shape the future of humanity.

Dialogue of the Poet and the Supreme Leader

Characters

THE POET
HIS WIFE
HIS FATHER
THE SUPREME LEADER

CHORUS

MAN 1
MAN 2
MAN 3
WOMAN 1
WOMAN 2
WOMAN 3

THREE FRIENDS
WAITER
PEOPLE IN A CAFE
SOLDIERS

Stage Directions

The stage will be dark. Gradually, an area at stage right will be illuminated. The Poet appears seated on a stool. Although he looks older, he is 35. The director may use whatever props he or she considers appropriate, but the set must be very simple: black cyclorama, platforms at different levels, and the furniture needed in the different scenes.

POET: *(As if awakening from a dream, smiling.)* Oh, yes! *(He begins to speak with emotion and happiness, as if he were reading one of his poems.)* One morning, in a foreign city, I had a revelation. The world was beautiful because the sun would always shine, and the trees would keep bearing fruit and offering shelter, and a girl would play on some balcony, and nothing would prevent the flocks of birds from brightening the golden sky. It was one of those cool and serene summer days which leave their mark on human beings. I wondered if there were a more concrete way of immortalizing all this beauty other than in the poem my imagination had conceived. In other words, if it weren't possible that the warmth, the light, and the happy sounds of this day could live forever in the hearts of all men. *(Pause. The Poet's face reveals a profound sadness. There is a marked transition from the almost euphoric happiness with which he has pronounced the last few words and this new expression of sorrow. Some clapping of hands is heard. The Poet seems not to have heard it. The clapping is repeated, louder. The Poet comes out of his daydream, startled. He smiles.)* Then I used to travel a lot, and everywhere I found harshness and cruelty. All that hurt me in an absurd way. Absurd? Why not? Wasn't the world absurd? My sorrow was not. And I tried to smile, just to find out if I could smooth out the harshness or what I believed was the harshness . . . *(The clapping is quite loud this time. The Poet, upset, bows his head.)* Pardon me, the harshness of mankind. I wrote many poems then, twisted and dark like charred trees. *(The clapping now becomes an approving applause. He stands up and bows dramatically. He walks about briefly, in silence. Then, he moves stage center. He finally laughs, childishly.)* In Rome, an old nun took me for a priest in layman's clothes and made me a part of her spiritual undertakings. Out of pity I didn't tell her her mistake. Afterwards, I had this longing for paradise which is, no doubt, the starting point for mystics. However, since I wasn't a mystic, this was a substitute for something else, or to use the words I'd repeat to myself in those days, the World's Eternal Summer. My country was ruled by a tyrant. Finally, I learned that a rebellion threatened his power, and he defended himself in desperation, flooding with blood the pockets of subversion . . . *(Clapping of disapproval is heard.)* The *Revolution* that . . . *(Clapping.)* A *heroic Revolution* that spread surprisingly fast. One night, tired, hungry—I was frequently hungry then, and sleep became a substitute for food since I seldom lacked a place to lie down—I went to bed after reading the headlines announcing the defeat of the rebellion. Needless to say, I couldn't sleep. That was like the catastrophic ending to all my dreams. But the next morning, new headlines restored my optimism. The . . . *(He hesitates, but smiles with sincere joy.)* Revolution had triumphed, and the tyrant and his clique had fled the country. An inner voice told me that my place was at home. A reassuring letter from my father finally convinced me, and I went back.

Applause in crescendo. The Poet salutes with conventional gestures of solidarity, holding his hands above his head and then moving his arms slightly. The spotlight that illuminated him is turned off while the applause continues to intensify. The light now focuses, stage front, on three men and three women wearing uniforms of the people's militia. Holding hands they recite or sing, Bertolt Brecht-fashion, a didactic hymn. Although this is definitely a parody, the actors and actresses must recite seriously.

MAN 1: We had a Revolution so that everyone would have bread and shoes!

WOMAN 1: We had a Revolution so that everyone would know the truth!

MAN 2: Farmers and workers, you're the Sons of the Revolution.

WOMAN 2: The Revolution fights against the mercenary politicians, against the greedy rich, against God's merchants!

MAN 3: That's why we have to defend the Revolution with all we've got, even if we must die doing so.

WOMAN 3: Tyrants of the world, beware of that day when the Revolution will triumph everywhere.

ALL: Long live the courageous militia and the Supreme Leader of the Revolution.

The lights go off. Another area stage rear is lighted. Three men are sitting at a table, drinking coffee, and talking very softly. Though the audience will not be able to make out what they are saying, their faces will reflect in turn anguish, anger, and sadness. The chair with its back to the audience remains empty. The Poet enters, greets the three men amiably, although his words should not be heard by the audience, and sits in the empty chair. A waiter approaches and takes his order, returning with a cup of coffee. The waiter's question and the Poet's order will also be given in a very low voice. The spectators should get the impression that the whole scene is being observed from afar, thus making it impossible to hear the voices of the men in the group. From the moment the Poet enters, the three men restrain themselves, showing caution and discretion in everything they say. They will talk less, pausing longer between their comments, and force themselves to smile politely as they converse with the Poet. Suddenly, something the Poet says, underscored by a movement of his arm in the air, provokes an abrupt reaction in one of the men whose face contracts in anger. He hits the table with his fist. The others attempt to calm him down. The Poet says something else and stands up. The first man also stands up, and the others follow suit. The latter two, who agree with the first man, rebuke the Poet. The Poet remains motionless, as if petrified in disbelief at the action of the men. Some curious bystanders have approached the group. All of a sudden, the Poet shouts as loud as he can, with a passion that makes everyone tremble: "Long live the Revolution!" Some of the bystanders join him repeating "Long live the Revolution!" Whereupon several soldiers enter and, guided by the bystanders, detain the three men who have been isolated in a corner. Now paralyzed by the unexpected turn of events, they are too surprised to comprehend fully the horror of their situation and its frightening consequences. The lights go off. Shouts of "Long live the Revolution!", fragments of undecipherable speeches, revolutionary mottos, and applause are heard. When the noise stops, stage left is lighted. A woman, about thirty, noble and proud looking, is sitting in a rocking chair. She wears very simple clothes of a single dark color. She rocks restlessly, reading a book off and on and staring sadly into space. Each time she does so, she stares longer into the void. The Poet enters.

POET: *(Without much enthusiasm.)* Hi.
WOMAN: *(Sad.)* Hi. *(Pause.)* Did you see him?
POET: No, I couldn't.
WOMAN: What are you going to do?

POET: *(After a pause, somewhat annoyed.)* And what do you want me to do?

WOMAN: *(Standing up.)* Act like a man. You can do something. They respect you . . . still.

POET: *(Somewhat irritated.)* I don't know what you mean by that *still.*

WOMAN: You know quite well what I mean. Don't play dumb. For some time now you've not been frank with me. But don't forget that, to use your very words, I have the rare gift of reading your thoughts. Although now there's no need of this rare gift of mine. Watch out for those who can do you harm.

POET: You're becoming a nuisance. *(He looks at her, immediately regretting what he has said in anger.)*

WOMAN: That's exactly what I wanted to hear you say.

POET: Forgive me.

WOMAN: Don't be foolish. You haven't offended me. Those things no longer affect me. But what you've said to me, in anger, is true in a more profound way. Because you refuse to face reality, I've become a nuisance, as have many others whose companionship you sought before. It's not the others who've changed and become nuisances. You're the one who's changed.

POET: *(Ironic.)* Oh, really? And what exactly do you mean by that?

WOMAN: You're not being honest, and you know it.

POET: Have you any complaints about me? If you want I'll say it again. I've always loved you and I love you more than anyone else! There!

WOMAN: Don't change the subject. That's not what I'm talking about.

POET: You drive me up the wall.

WOMAN: I know. That's what I'm trying to accomplish, just to see if you come to your senses and realize what's happening to you. *(Pause in which they look at one another intensely. Finally, she turns away. What follows will be said with her back to the Poet, hiding from him the suffering that her face will reveal.)* I'm leaving, you know. *(He tries to approach her.)* No, please, listen to me. I'm in your way, and more so with each passing day. People can see the repugnance I feel in my face. If I don't talk it's only because I know that to do so would hurt you.

POET: But . . . will you go by yourself?

WOMAN: No, my parents are coming along. It'll be a matter of a few months.

POET: *(Touched by the news. Tense.)* It's a fact, then. Why didn't you tell me before?

WOMAN: *(Turning toward him.)* I was afraid you'd try to dissuade me. *(Again they look at one another intensely.)* I think it's best for us to separate as soon as possible. If I stay with you while I wait to get an exit visa, you'll have a lot to explain after I'm gone. *(About to cry.)* Don't you agree? *(Now the Poet is the one who turns away to avoid seeing her. She takes a few steps toward the exit and grabs a large shopping bag from a nearby table. He sits in the rocking chair and stares in the air.)* I have to go to the market. If I don't get in line today, our number won't come up again until Tuesday.

She leaves. He remains in the rocking chair with the same air of self-absorption and sadness which the woman had at the beginning of the scene. Lights go off. Several sounds are heard: the noise of the boots of marching soldiers and of rifles being readied to be fired, military commands, an order to fire shots, and finally, the scream of one who has been hit by the firing squad, followed by the shouts of "Death to the enemies of the Revolution!" The lights now illuminate an area stage right where a man, about sixty, well preserved, lies on a miserable cot in a cell. He has the dignified and modest look of one of those public employees who, thanks to their perseverance, make a career of their job in the public domain. He is the Poet's father. The Poet enters, escorted by a soldier who remains standing in the back of the cell.

POET: Dad! *(The father props himself up and offers him a hand. The Poet approaches his father. They shake hands.)* How are you?

FATHER: See for yourself. I can't complain.

POET: *(Pulling the only chair in the room closer to the bed.)* Do you need anything? They'll allow me to bring whatever you need.

FATHER: Well, my eyeglasses broke. See if you can get me another pair. The prescription's in the top drawer of my bureau. And I could use something to read . . . to kill time, you know. Nothing heavy.

POET: Anything to eat?

FATHER: No, no. Some tea, perhaps, if you can find any. It helps my stomach. *(Silence.)* Do you know how long they'll keep me here? *(The soldier is annoyed by this question.)*

POET: I don't know. *(He looks at the soldier who tries to ignore him.)* Can you leave us alone? They promised me . . .

SOLDIER: *(Impersonal.)* You have ten minutes. Those are my orders, in case you asked. *(He leaves.)*

POET: Dad, I've been told that you were involved in a conspiracy.

FATHER: *(Laughs, somewhat sarcastically.)* And you believed them?

POET: They say they have a formal accusation, that you got together with the others in a bar, and that you were plotting counterrevolutionary acts . . . some type of sabotage . . . It all seems weird to me, but since you've told me so many times that something was bound to happen, that things couldn't go on the way they were . . . A waiter was spying on you, and he was the one who blew the whistle.

FATHER: The waiter, of course! He was also the one who, before the triumph of the Revolution, brought coffee every morning to our office. He went all out to flatter the Secretary General and his men in order to get some decent tips. Why wouldn't he hate me, I, who witnessed the humiliation he had been subject to day after day? I'm sure he's at least a Secret Agent now.

POET: But what did you and your friends talk about?

FATHER: Do I have to tell you? About those things people have always discussed: the country, international politics, the government . . . and some criticism, of course. But to call those conversations a conspiracy . . .

POET: Was that all?

FATHER: *(Serious.)* I see you don't even trust your father any more.

POET: These are difficult times, Dad. Some things carelessly said can be harmful to the country.

FATHER: Nonsense. I don't think I know you. Why not call a spade a spade?

POET: *(Looking suspiciously at the door and standing up.)* Dad . . .

FATHER: For years I took the harassment and the corruption at work to make sure that you and your mother wouldn't lack the necessities. No one could have been happier than I was when it was announced that all that garbage was coming to an end. I myself, don't you remember, wrote the letter encouraging you to return from your exile abroad.

POET: Yes, yes. I know . . .

FATHER: Let me speak! At the beginning I was in favor of all this. Their intentions seemed good. There were things every decent person had dreamed about; some things I'd heard my sainted father talk about when I was a child. But you must come to terms with the fact that justice is not realized by means of injustice. The other day some militiamen kicked out of the entrance of our office building, a poor old man who sold candy in the lobby ever since I can remember, saying that private businesses were now forbidden. To say nothing about those shot to death on the spot if found trying to flee the country illegally. This and all other jails are overflowing with political prisoners. I've heard stories here that you wouldn't believe. And I know that some of these prisoners were true revolutionaries and, deep inside, still are.

POET: There are many traitors, Dad.

FATHER: Whom have they betrayed? . . . A bunch of people who rule our lives in the name of a justice so obscure that no one knows what it is? I welcomed rationing until I found out that the leaders, Supreme as well as Minimal ones, always had meat on their tables.

POET: Dad. *(He looks at the door.)*

FATHER: In the meantime, my neighbor's all skin and bones from taking food out of her mouth to feed her son. And if I can't get it off my chest talking, the best thing for me would be to leave the country, provided an execution doesn't put an end to my present predicament first.

POET: Don't say those things, Dad. Everything'll be straightened out. They're investigating, and if things are the way you say, you'll be set free. Remember the times we live in. We're threatened by a possible invasion. There are real counterrevolutionary groups that don't share your idealism and that take action against our system . . . Please, understand.

FATHER: I only understand that you're afraid. Not afraid of others but of yourself. You're afraid to admit the failure of your ideals, more strongly rooted in you, perhaps, than in me. I'm old and I've seen so much that I can assure you that the perfect system you and the other dreamers like you have imagined, doesn't exist and never will.

POET: I've never seen you so pessimistic.

FATHER: Man's truth has been revealed to me in this cell. I wish it hadn't. And I can tell you that when man lets himself be ruled by his evil side, he's the worst of animals. Beasts are cruel to each other in order to survive, but man always justifies his cruelty with moral principles he merely invents.

POET: *(After an embarrassing silence.)* Perhaps it's so, but I can't give up my longing for perfection. If this isn't the answer, we'll have to look for another one.

The Father looks at him in admiration and astonishment. He is going to speak but he sees such purity in his son's eyes that he refrains from doing so and lies down again on the cot, looking tired. The Poet approaches him.

POET: *(Lovingly.)* Take care. I'll bring the things you need. But I'm sure you won't be here long. *(The soldier enters and announces that the visiting time is over.)* So long.

FATHER: So long, son. Forget my last few words. I'm nothing more than a prosaic old man. *(The Poet smiles and leaves, followed by the soldier. The lights go off.)*

At stage left, Man 1 and Woman 1, sitting on high stools, sing or recite, alternating lines.

I praise the summer of the world,
the overwhelming music of the birds,
the laughter of the girl at play,
the trees, bearing fruit and flower.
This is the time to live
to bring about an era for the rest,
when winter's gone and man is at his best,
without the burdens of pitiful old age.
The sun'll warm up the world,
its crops, its peoples and hearts,
and together they'll praise this life
where summer lives never to die.
A New Man will write the legend,
a simple story which is his very own,
for with a smile on his face, flower in hand,
this New Man will, one day, be born.
He will be pure, he will be strong,
and you, comrade, praise with me the joy
of our unity in labor and in trust

until the birds announce that He has come
and the summer is crowned in our sky of gold.

Lights go off. When the lights come on, the Poet is standing, handcuffed, as if waiting for something or someone. There is a soldier with a machine gun hanging from his shoulder, stage rear. The Supreme Leader enters from the right, wearing a guerrilla uniform without any medals or distinctive ornaments. The humble outfit and demeanor, perhaps sincere, hide an iron will and a pride which is common to military men in power. The Supreme Leader takes a few steps and looks the Poet in the eye. He offers him his hand, but immediately realizes that the Poet is handcuffed, so he makes a sign to the soldier who removes the handcuffs and then returns to his place. The Supreme Leader motions him to leave. Finally, he walks toward the Poet, arms outstretched to embrace him. The Poet, confused, lets himself be hugged.

SUPREME LEADER: This is how I wanted to see you, face to face. It's time to put down the weapons. I know that you and I understand one another like two old friends. I know you've not betrayed the Revolution but that the Revolution has been unjust to you.

POET: That's very true. I know that we really understand one another . . . However, under the present circumstances . . . I think this cell is the only place left for me in the Revolution.

SUPREME LEADER: I don't know what you mean. I've come to get you out of here, to take you back to the job of building our Revolution. I accept the fact that you've been mistreated, that your aloof behavior and some poems that say hardly anything that the Revolution could *censure*, do not deserve such harsh treatment. I'm sorry I couldn't be in charge of this whole matter personally.

POET: . . . that the Revolution could *censure*. That's the issue. What's to be censured? Why censure anything? If I had written truly reprehensible things, would I have the option you're offering me now? Would I be released?

SUPREME LEADER: The Revolution—I thought you understood this—can't allow the slightest offense against it. If I have to keep one hundred poets in prison so that they don't attack the Revolution, subtly or otherwise, I will.

POET: That's the problem, I tell you. Either we're free to express ourselves in any way we choose in a society that calls itself free, or we're subject to another type of tyranny, because tyranny comes in many forms.

SUPREME LEADER: Are you telling me about tyrannies, I, who fought five years to overthrow the most odious one we ever had? No, what I propose isn't tyranny but the well-being of the majority to the detriment of the minority that didn't want to give up a single one of its many comforts.

POET: I gave up my few comforts a long time ago. In any case, it isn't a matter of comforts, but one of freedom.

SUPREME LEADER: Very well, freedom . . . Is it too much to ask that a few sacrifice in order to keep alive the revolutionary enthusiasm of the masses? If the slightest discontent is planted among the people, in the long run the work of the Revolution could come crumbling down. And the workers and the peasants, blinded for just one instant, would lose all we've given them: economic security and personal dignity.

POET: But, do you really think that discontent can be sowed, that one or a hundred poems can accomplish that? I doubt very much that the workers and peasants even read our poems.

SUPREME LEADER: Then why do you write them? So that the counter-revolution can make use of them abroad? So that certain groups can talk about persecution? *(Pause.)* We can't take any chances.

POET: *(Thinking.)* What I'm trying to tell you is that the people's discontent is a spontaneous thing. It's not created by any external factor.

SUPREME LEADER: The counterrevolution is quite clever. It infiltrates into everything. I can't imagine the people's discontent being anything but the result of the doings of agents trying to belittle what we've achieved in the past few years.

POET: But what has been achieved? And what a price we've all had to pay.

SUPREME LEADER: Do I have to spell it out for you? You know what the Revolution has done in the countryside in these ten years. I'm sure you remember the children with big bellies, bloated by intestinal parasites, living with their families in huts with earthen floors and with no schools to attend. You know this has all been changed. Everyone now eats and dresses decently. The literacy brigades took the written word everywhere. Education now reaches all. Infant mortality is almost nonexistent. What more do you want? *(Pompous.)* What more do you and the rest of the blubbering poets want?

POET: *(Harsh, bitter.)* We're tormented by the regulations that control every single aspect of our lives. The Revolution has left nothing to man's imagination.

SUPREME LEADER: Imagination! We can't achieve our goals with . . . *imagination.* He who insists on imagination may as well leave this land and starve in a far away place.

POET: You see? We can't agree. You don't listen to me. You refuse to understand.

SUPREME LEADER: The Revolution, any revolution, needs laws, regulations, stability, *reason.*

POET: Including those secret councils of informers devoted solely to spying and making their accusations . . . and sending honest persons to jail, as happened to my father?

SUPREME LEADER: Your father, if I'm not mistaken, left the country a long time ago. It's normal to make mistakes in situations as difficult as ours. I've made every effort to enforce true justice in the case of accusations. Those who are behind bars today were fairly judged, found guilty, and sentenced.

POET: *(Bitter, without irony, beginning to look weak.)* Even me?

SUPREME LEADER: Your case is something different. A mutual and lamentable misunderstanding. That's why I'm here, in person, to vindicate you.

POET: *(Sincerely, favorably surprised.)* But, do you really want to set me free? After all I've said?

SUPREME LEADER: I understand more than you think. Yes, I've come to set you free. I know you share our ideals of the Revolution; that can't be wiped out in a day. For many years you were a good revolutionary. You're part of the Revolution; only within the Revolution could you really be happy. Think about all we've discussed. Haven't you spoken freely? But I hope you'll also consider all I've said and keep it in mind. You aren't, you can't be selfish. Think of the others, the people you've praised in your poems in their peaceful activities as well as their heroic struggle against the counterrevolutionary invasion. Not long ago you wrote, "The Revolution is necessary."

POET: *(He has listened to the above speech with his head bowed, thoughtful.)* Could we . . . perhaps . . . ?

SUPREME LEADER: Ask whatever you want. We can come to an understanding.

POET: Could we, I mean the other "blubbering poets" and I *(He says this with a certain humor; he is not bitter.)*, meet with you in private to talk over the possibilities and problems of our work?

SUPREME LEADER: Whenever you wish. You have my word.

POET: Am I a free man, then?

SUPREME LEADER: Not yet. I have a request to make of you.

POET: Yes.

SUPREME LEADER: It's important that what you admit in private be known publicly. This will do you and the Revolution much good.

POET: A retraction?

SUPREME LEADER: No, a reiteration of your old revolutionary principles.

POET: Very well. But not here. O.K.? I can attend to that as soon as I take care of a number of things of mine pending outside.

SUPREME LEADER: Yes, here. *(He draws a piece of paper from his jacket pocket and gives it to the Poet.)*

POET: *(Looking at the piece of paper in disgust.)* Oh! You've already written it . . .

SUPREME LEADER: It's easier this way.

POET: . . . and following the Revolutionary Party's line. I see.

SUPREME LEADER: All you have to do is sign it.

POET: And if I don't?

SUPREME LEADER: Then . . .

POET: I remain in prison . . .

SUPREME LEADER: If you refuse to do something as simple as this, then we'll all have to question your revolutionary beliefs.

POET: Maybe I'm a truer revolutionary than many in the Party.

SUPREME LEADER: It's up to you. Think about it; take your time. I can understand your wanting to reflect on all of this. A delegate will come in an hour to pick up the signed document. *(He starts to leave, then turns around.)* We trust in your good judgment. *(He leaves.)*

POET: *(He looks at the piece of paper, sits on a bench, and reads the paper fully. He looks ahead at the audience. It is a fixed, troubled stare.*

Finally he stands up.) So be it. *(He begins to tear the document very slowly as the lights start to dim.)*

CURTAIN

Olofé's Razor

Matías Montes Huidobro

Matías Montes Huidobro

Born in Sagua la Grande, Province of Las Villas, in 1931, Matías Montes Huidobro is one of the most prolific Cuban playwrights in exile. Before leaving the island in 1961, where he earned a doctorate in education from the University of Havana, Montes was active as an educator, a playwright, and a theater critic for the newspaper *Revolución* as well as for national television. In 1950 his play *Las cuatro brujas* received honorable mention in a national drama contest sponsored by the group Prometeo. The following year he received first prize in this competition for his work, *Sobre las mismas rocas*. *Los acosados*, published by *Lunes de Revolución* and staged in Havana in 1959, was presented on national television in 1960. *La botija*, appearing about the same time, was published in the review *Casa de las Américas* in 1961. *Las vacas*, which won the Premio José Antonio Ramos in 1960, was staged in Havana's Palacio de Bellas Artes a year later. Additional dramatic pieces by Montes include: *El tiro por la culata* (*Teatro Estudio*, Havana, 1961), *Gas en los poros* (Supplement of *Lunes de Revolución*, Havana, 1961), and *La sal de los muertos* (written in 1961 and published in O. Rodríguez-Sardiñas and C. M. Suárez Radillo, *Teatro Contemporáneo Hispanoamericano*, Madrid: Escelicer, 1971.) Montes has written many plays in exile, a number of which have appeared in various anthologies and journals. A noted scholar, poet, and novelist as well, Montes Huidobro is presently Professor of Spanish at the University of Hawaii.

Written in 1981 and published in the original Spanish in the literary journal *Prismal/Cabral* in 1982, *Olofé's Razor* (*La navaja de Olofé*) was successfully staged in Miami by the theater group Teatro Nuevo in 1986. In presenting the important Black cultural stratum of Cuban society, this play combines the topic of Hispanic machismo with that of Afro-Cuban myths. The main characters, two mulattoes, live ruled by their belief in two main Yoruba gods, Changó and Olofé.

Changó, god of thunder, had many lovers. He also lived connubially with his aunt, Ochún, and unknowingly was about to bed his own mother. The son of the female protagonist, whom the Woman calls "my little Changó," is doubly possessed by Changó and Olofé, and commits incest with his mother. Olofé, who according to legend decided to keep away from humans, descends, through the art of the creator, from heaven to possess all the characters in turn. Montes portrays him as the symbol of absolute virility whom every human would like to emulate. His importance can be reduced to the efficacy of his genitals. In this play, where reality, fiction, and myth intermingle, the Woman's lover cuts off the genitals of the incarnate god and puts them on, thus assuming the personality of the god and enhancing his own masculinity. Even the Woman covets Olofé's genitals. If she had them, she could realize the freedom and power of this magnificent creature. Moreover, she would possess the male organ that would assure her the sensual pleasure which she no longer enjoys, since men ignore her because of her age. It is the Woman who finally fulfills all of her needs as she performs the symbolic execution which also gives her the desired revenge against the lover who had betrayed her.

Olofé's Razor

Characters

A MAN
A WOMAN

Setting

The action takes place in the city of Santiago de Cuba, during Mardi Gras, sometime in the first half of the twentieth century. At stage rear, a traditional Cuban door which combines horizontal blinds and an upper arch made of stained glass sections in different colors. The set will be divided into three well-defined areas which will clarify in most instances the relationship between the two characters as they move from one area to another. Since each character portrays a variety of personae, *his or her place on stage at a given time should help the audience to identify those* personae *and to follow the abrupt changes that occasionally occur in the characters as they move from one* persona *to the next.*

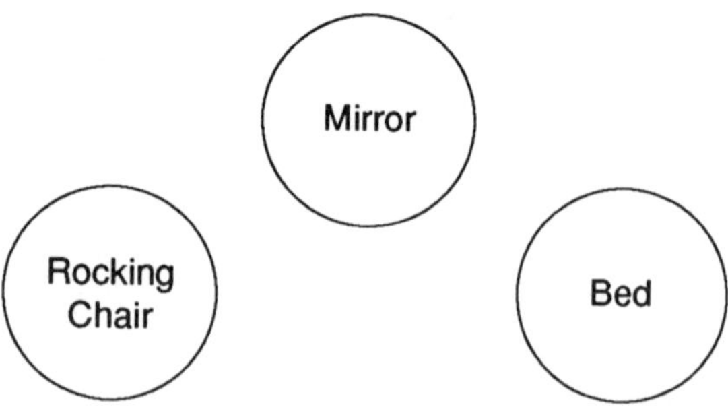

A large mirror at stage center will be the focal point of the action. This is the man's narcissistic area. As the curtain rises, he will be partially dressed while shaving with a large old-fashioned straight razor. He will never complete getting dressed, an act which should be seen as an unfulfilled ritual. The director may suggest this in any way he chooses. At one point, the man will shine his two-tone shoes which are on a small table next to the mirror. There could also be a clothes tree with a shirt and a pair of pants in a striking white. The mirror area will serve both the man and the woman for their self-adoration. Both are mulattoes. He is twenty. She is around forty. At times she will look attractive, at others, she will seem prematurely aged.

Whenever the woman plays the role of the mother she will move to the rocking chair area. To play the lover, she will go to the bed area. The front of the stage and the mirror area can be used as transition spaces. In the background, the drum beats and the music for the dancing formations which parade down the street during Mardi Gras in Santiago de Cuba are heard. The fireworks outside could illuminate the scene from time to time.

WOMAN: *(Surprised, as she enters.)* Are you leaving? Getting dressed already?

MAN: Can't you see I am? What else would I be doing?

WOMAN: You don't have to leave; my old man isn't back yet. He's probably getting drunk in the corner bar.

MAN: So?

WOMAN: *(She approaches and caresses him.)* Nothing . . .

MAN: Nothing. That's exactly what I tell *you*.

WOMAN: *(In the same way.)* Nothing . . . Honey . . . *(She moves away and throws herself on the bed.)* Come on . . . Let's do it again . . . We still have time . . .

MAN: *(He looks at her hesitantly and then continues to shave.)* No, damn it! Stop acting like a whore!

WOMAN: *(She stays in bed for a moment as though in ecstasy. Then sits up, fusses with her hair, looks at the rocking chair, and stands up.)* Santiago's jumping tonight. It's real hot! Changó in person has come down from heaven to drive all the women wild. The streets of Santiago are so crowded you can't walk. *(She dances as she sings:)*

Oculé Mayá, oculé Mayá,[1]
Where are you, where are you, black man?

Oculé Mayá, oculé Mayá,
Where are you going, black man?
Oculé Mayá, oculé Mayá . . .

She approaches the rocking chair and, without sitting down, rocks it as she sings a lullaby:

Sleep, sleep, my little Changó,
I'm your mother,
Yemanyá, who loves you so,
Even though I know
That one day by mistake
You'll try to take
Your own mother to bed . . .

Sleep, sleep, my little Changó,
Ochún the goddess
Wants to know where you went
Because she knows that one day
Once you're grown, in her bed
You'll teach her the secrets
And true pleasures of sex.

(She sits in the rocking chair.) Be careful, son. Don't drink too much tonight, and watch out with that razor.

MAN: Stories, Mom, stories . . .

WOMAN: The type of life you're leading is shaped like a knife. Olofé himself, wearing a butterfly suit told me so. *(She sings:)*

Sleep, sleep, my little Changó,
Yemanyá has a present for you . . .
Sleep, sleep, my little one,
Sleep tight while I sing to you . . .

MAN: Since when does Olofé put on a butterfly costume? Maybe it's on account of Mardi Gras. People go wild during these celebrations. And me too, although I don't go crazy. Tell Olofé to disguise himself as an old black man.

WOMAN: The celebration . . . The conga . . . The rumba . . . The drum beats . . .

MAN: Everyone must go out and join in the fun! No one can stay home!

WOMAN: I don't have to, sweetheart, because I'm really Olofé, the Almighty, dressed up as an old black woman.

MAN: This is a special day to rejoice, a day like no other . . .

WOMAN: Not for me it isn't. I'm old and finished. *(All of a sudden she falls on her knees, raises her arms and shouts:)* Olofé, Olofé, get me out of this pit where you've put me. *(There is a grotesque transition as she approaches on her knees the man who is in the mirror area. She sings, bizarrely:)*

You see, you see, I can't walk.
You see, you see, I can't fuck.
I'm a black woman who can't suck.
I'm a black woman without a cock.

MAN: I'm going to piss all over you.

WOMAN: *(Crawling and reaching the bed.)* Olofé . . . Olofé . . . I'm a black woman without a cock! *(Transition, laughing.)* Olofé was so beautiful when he was coming down from heaven through the clouds, stark naked . . . His mother was in one of the clouds getting ready to drop some rain on the earth, and she said to him crying: "If you don't cover up your dingy, Olofé, the dogs'll eat it." And Olofé didn't believe her because his father had told him: "Listen, Olofé, don't pay any attention to your mother's advice because the cock never dies. It's like the tail of a small lizard. When you cut it off, it keeps on moving." And Olofé became the master of the world and his mother, Mama Olofé, wept, and that's why it began to rain and water appeared on this earth. But Olofé laughed at the water! *(As in a trance, the man stops shaving and looks at the woman in the mirror.)* A mountain that had been split in two by a valley said to Olofé: "Come, Olofé! I am the earth, she who has everything. Look at these two mounds, Olofé, you luscious man, you pimp, who knows how to use your tongue so well. Look at these two mounds, at these two breasts, Olofé!" And the earth caressed her own breasts. In a cloud which was really a mirror, Olofé could see the earth's reflection, and he looked over the mounds, and down into the valley, offering itself. He got so excited that he finally had to come down.

MAN: *(Turning toward the woman.)* What was the earth like?

WOMAN: Just as it is now. Come here, Olofé, you doll of palm trees, my sugarcane sweetheart, my lover of rum and molasses! Come here, Olofé, so that you can relive that feeling of doing it with the earth . . . Do you remember, Olofé? Try to remember, you savory black man . . .

MAN: Olofé?

WOMAN: Earth.

MAN: *(Now on the bed, next to her.)* Olofé?

WOMAN: *(Together in bed.)* Olofé, he who was everything! Come, touch me, Olofé! I am Olofé. You are Olofé! The bed is Olofé! Olofé! Olofé! Olofé has it all and gives it all as well! He takes and gives! He loves and lets himself be loved! He goes up and down! He kisses and lets himself be kissed! He runs and jumps! He touches and lets himself be touched! He sings and dances! He smells and lets himself be smelled! He eats and lets himself be eaten! You're Olofé! I'm Olofé! He flies and swims! He swims in the water! *(She lets her head fall back and he is about to kiss her. The position is that of a sexual act, but somewhat distorted. Her head hangs over the bed. She adds in anguish:)* He swims . . . in . . . the water . . . !

MAN: *(He raises his torso, still on top of her, showing his naked chest. Still in this position he says:)* He swims . . . in . . . the water . . . ! *(He gets up, moves to the mirror, and looks at himself in it.)* I am Olofé!

WOMAN: How time flies! *(Getting up.)* It seems it was only yesterday. I still remember when you played ball and I took you to school, which you never liked. *(She is sitting on the edge of the bed. She stands up and walks toward the rocking chair.)* Oh, son, how my legs ache! *(She gets closer to the rocking chair and sings sadly:)*

Oculé Mayá, oculé Mayá,
Where are you, where are you, black man?
Oculé Mayá, oculé Mayá,
Where are you going, black man?
Oculé Mayá, oculé Mayá . . .

(She lets herself fall in the rocking chair.) I still remember that teacher . . . what was her name? Juana María? She always came to complain about you . . . And it all seems like only yesterday. But no, it all happened a long time ago, didn't it?

MAN: I don't know. I don't remember.

WOMAN: And now you're a full grown man. Be careful. Those women are driving you crazy.

MAN: Don't start all over again.

WOMAN: *(Angry, in a low voice.)* The old folks end up cooking, doing the dishes and the dirty laundry . . . while the rest go dance and make out.

MAN: That's life.

WOMAN: Nowadays women aren't good, my son. Watch out.

MAN: They're the ones who have to watch out for me.

WOMAN: My mother was right; one's own children are always thankless.

MAN: Look, old woman, I'm not going to be tied to your apron strings forever.

WOMAN: Watch out, son. Those mulatto girls who undress so easily are pure fire and you could get burned. I've been telling you so for a long time. Youngsters, youngsters!

MAN: *(Looking at the woman, ironically.)* I'm sure I could find someone who's no longer a spring chicken.

WOMAN: *(Standing, irritated by his remark, still next to the rocking chair.)* What exactly do you mean by that?

MAN: You know darn well what I mean.

WOMAN: Why do I have to put up with all this? Damn it! The old folks have to baby-sit their grandchildren while the others go out and have a ball. *(With nostalgia. She walks to the mirror.)* It's been such a long time . . . Those nights . . . the saint would possess me . . . We drank pure alcohol with just a few drops of lemon. Ah! If you could have seen your mother in those days, son! It's so sad to see oneself like this! But if I were young, I'd be enjoying myself, you know? In my day I was great. I would have been just another one of . . . *those* . . . Yes, it was so long ago . . . I still remember when you took your first step. You were such a cute little mulatto; everyone loved playing with you. And you spent all your time with me. When you were afraid of something, you'd come and hide under my skirts . . . You probably learned a lot hiding in there. Then it was I who danced in the streets during Mardi Gras . . . Then it was I who enjoyed looking at myself in the mirror. *(The man, in bed, will let himself be influenced by the woman's talk as if he could also remember all of this on a double level, both as child and man.)* That night . . . my husband, my old man wasn't home and you had fallen asleep in my bed because you were afraid, and you snuggled very close to me . . . Then someone knocked at the door . . . I think I heard someone whistle . . . and you were sleeping like an angel . . . I didn't want to open the door . . . I knew it couldn't be my old man because he was getting drunk in the corner bar . . . It was a gentle knock, and each time I heard it, I felt caresses over my entire body as if whoever was at the door could get to my body even before entering. He had been looking at me for quite a while, you know, in the grocery store, at Panchita's fruit stand . . . I don't know . . . And he'd . . . he'd whisper in my ear those filthy remarks of his . . . which I enjoyed so much. And after that, after he got me all excited, I had to resign myself to coming home all alone. I'd take you in my arms and start singing: "Sleep, sleep, my little Changó . . ." But this didn't help. I just couldn't get him off my mind. Whatever I did to forget about him was useless because, whether he was looking at me or not, his stare had entered my body and it caressed me from within whenever it pleased. *(She is looking at the man—now her son—in the mirror. She turns and walks toward the bed.)* Then I got up, being careful not to wake you up, and walked to the door. But I didn't really have to open it because I knew he was already inside. I realized he was here in the bedroom, in bed. When I finally opened the door, there he was, Olofé, in the flesh, more handsome than ever, more handsome than how I'd pictured him in my dreams. Because the man in front of me wasn't the one I had seen in the grocery store. No, he was none other than Olofé. And he began to say all those things you've heard me say so many times: "Come, touch me, Olofé! I am Olofé! You are Olofé!" *(The position is similar to the previous one, only that now the roles have been switched and it is the woman who is on top of the man. The man has his head hanging over the bed. She is beautiful. She raises her torso as she shouts:)* I am Olofé!

MAN: *(Pulling away brusquely.)* You *were* Olofé. That's all finished.

WOMAN: *(Pause. She sings sadly:)*

Oculé Mayá, oculé Mayá,
Black woman, where are you hiding?
Oculé Mayá, oculé Mayá,
Black woman, where are you going?
Oculé Mayá, oculé Mayá . . .

The old folks end up cooking, doing the dishes and the dirty laundry . . . while the rest go dance and make out.

MAN: *(Singing in a different key:)*

Oculé Mayá, oculé Mayá,
Black woman, where are you hiding?
Oculé Mayá, oculé Mayá,
Black woman, where are you going?
Oculé Mayá, oculé Mayá . . .

WOMAN: I'm fed up with all this, you know? I'm sick and tired of your getting me all excited and then leaving me to go to bed with who knows who.

MAN: Come now, stop being jealous. You know you're the only one I love.

WOMAN: You're such an arrogant rooster . . . I know darn well that you lie to me, as if I were the oldest hen in your coop.

MAN: Now, baby, don't get mad at your sweetheart.

WOMAN: *(In the rocking chair.)* The old folks end up cooking, doing the dishes and the dirty laundry . . . while the rest go dance and make out. The memories . . . The pots and pans . . . The shouting . . . The grandchildren . . .

MAN: Tonight I'll make the most beautiful grandchildren you've ever seen, just for you. In nine months, the hens of Santiago will start laying gigantic eggs from which beautiful reddish roosters will hatch.

WOMAN: Oh yeah? You skunk! If you think I'm gonna be looking after the children of all those bitches, you've got another thing coming. I just won't take it.

MAN: No kidding. I bet in no time at all you'll be spoiling them and getting them under your skirt, just like you did with me.

WOMAN: You're dead wrong. I'm so old that I'm not even good enough for that anymore. I'm an old hag. My hands have calluses from working so hard to bring you up. What a miserable life. Why are one's children so ungrateful?

MAN: You still have what it takes. Why don't you go dancing with your old man?

WOMAN: My old man?

MAN: You'll have to make do with him. What choice do you have?

WOMAN: Olofé?

MAN: Now what? I think you've gone bananas.

WOMAN: My old man! He's not Olofé.

MAN: The hell with Olofé. Olofé this, Olofé that. Damn it! Your old man *is* Olofé.

WOMAN: *(Stands up.)* I'm gonna slap you!

MAN: Come on now, smile . . . and don't try to scare me. I'm too old for that. I'm leaving so as to put an end to this nonsense.

WOMAN: No, this isn't the way you used to treat me. I can't . . . Yes, I can understand . . . I'm fat, ugly and fat like an old pig. Fat and flabby. You don't want me anymore . . .

MAN: Don't be that way . . . Of course I love you. You're my angel.

And if you don't like your old man anymore, there're other men besides me out there.

WOMAN: What man'd want to be with me? Don't you realize what has happened to me? I gave you my youth. Don't, don't laugh. You know darn well that here, in bed at midnight, I'm still something else . . . The old man! How dare you say such things?

MAN: Because it's gotten into your head that I'm Olofé, and it's just not so. Look around and you'll find many more like me, even younger and more inexperienced, and you could teach them. Perhaps you could teach one of them how to be Olofé. Think about it. The old man is senile and won't care who you bring home.

WOMAN: But *I* care. It won't be that easy to put an end to what we have, because when I played him dirty with you . . .

MAN: With me . . . and with the guy next door . . . and with every other man in the neighborhood.

WOMAN: With you or with whomever . . . They wouldn't leave me alone for a second. Not even Mardi Gras would drive them away from me . . . But with you it's different. How dare you go out there and teach those other women what you learned with me!

MAN: *(He sings:)*

Oculé Mayá, oculé Mayá,
Black woman, where are you going?
Oculé Mayá, oculé Mayá . . .

WOMAN: Sure, sing, dance, have fun. Make fun of me, go on, sing that tune again: "Black woman, where are you hiding?" But listen, lover boy, one can hear that same story every single day in Pancho's grocery store, in Felipe's butcher shop, in Paulina's five-and-ten. In the afternoon soaps . . . The marquis's wife goes to bed with the senator . . . and with her chauffeur . . . The pimp who climbs the social ladder and becomes a politician . . . The gynecologist who takes the countess, her daughter, and even his nurse to bed. The lawyer who has an affair with his secretary. The young virgin who was deflowered during an unexpected visit from the tamale vendor. I'm telling you . . . it happens every single day. And then, "bye, bye . . ." and if I bump into you again, I'll pretend we never met and keep on walking. Haven't you told me all of this many times? I know the story by heart. The jealousy scene. Maybe you got the mayor's daughter pregnant by mistake. You know darn well how it goes. She comes from a nice family and all that. You both lost your heads, and then . . . what can you do? You made fun of my old man first by going to bed with me, and now you're making fun of me by going to bed with others. Don't admit it if you don't want to . . . There're mirrors around here, you know? I can see myself, lover boy, you cheap pimp. You ridiculed him first and now it's my turn to be humiliated. Perfect: the cuckold, the betrayed mistress, and the pimp who'd go to bed for a buck and end up as a wealthy and respectable citizen. Quite a story, isn't it? Great plot for a soap.

MAN: My mother wouldn't feed me.

WOMAN: But when the baby got hold of her breast, he'd suck all of her milk, down to the very last drop.

MAN: And then there was the other guy who kept her from feeding me. He'd come and keep her busy any time, in the middle of the morning, at night . . . and I was always hungry.

WOMAN: That's not so. My old man . . .

MAN: No, it wasn't your husband. It was Olofé. *(He sings:)*

Oculé Mayá, oculé Mayá,
Black woman, where are you hiding?
Oculé Mayá, oculé Mayá,
Black woman, where are you going?
Oculé Mayá, oculé Mayá . . .

WOMAN: Not now, Olofé, the baby's asleep . . .

MAN: The son of a bitch! I was the one you were betraying. He'd dare show up in front of me and let me see him stark naked with a hard on.

WOMAN: *(Jokingly.)* Come on, don't be jealous. You know you're the only one I love.

MAN: Until that night when I cut off his . . .

WOMAN: That night? I don't understand, Olofé. What do you mean?

MAN: It was all so easy. *(Approaching the bed.)* He was singing on his way here, so I heard him coming. Besides, he was already inside you . . .

WOMAN: You were such a smart baby! You know, I suspected something because you loved being kissed a lot. So you were Olofé, weren't you? Weren't you?

MAN: I wasn't asleep. I was in bed, about to wake up. When he began to whistle that tune of "Black woman, where are you hiding," I let him whistle with my own lips.

WOMAN: You? That's why he was so close to me. But how come he didn't realize what was going on?

MAN: He didn't because he was having so much fun that the more I enjoyed myself, the more he thought he was Olofé.

WOMAN: That's filthy!

MAN: *(He is now in bed.)* Can't you see? If I was doing it with you, then I was the one making fun of Olofé . . .

WOMAN: How dumb I was. How could I not realize what was happening? In the hands of you men, we women are toys.

MAN: You could hear him so close to you, and slowly he slipped into you. I could feel everything because Olofé had penetrated your body and I was now Olofé, and the air we breathed in the room was filled with the smell of Olofé.

WOMAN: You're crazy! That's nothing but a bunch of lies! Good grief! Your black grandmother must have been stuffing your head again with her African superstitions. A bunch of lies. But even though she is black, ebony black, doesn't your white, holy, Catholic, and apostolic grandfather count? How can you possibly take seriously all that junk about Olofé?

MAN: When you finally fell asleep . . .

WOMAN: No way. Who was singing the lullaby, you or me? And besides, in those days you were just a tiny baby. I bathed you, and I knew how small you were. No way, I tell you. There's no way you could have been Olofé . . .

MAN: *(Opening the razor and placing it on the woman's neck.)* I knew that, but I had the razor, and whoever had the razor was going to become Olofé!

WOMAN: Lies! That can't be!

MAN: I'd looked at myself in the mirror and had seen Olofé instead. He had what I wanted! *(He caresses her with the blade.)*

WOMAN: *(Laughing.)* No, it was I who wanted to have what Olofé had. *(She caresses him until she gets hold of the razor. From this point on, they will play with the razor, taking it from one another, being either sexual or threatening, as the director sees fit.)*

MAN: That night he did what he always did when he came into the room. As usual, he was naked. He couldn't waste time taking off his clothes.

WOMAN: True. That was a bad habit of his.

MAN: When I opened the door, everything was dark. Because I'd been with you, your scent, which was in me, was at the same time Olofé's scent. Don't you see? We couldn't tell one from the other.

WOMAN: Next thing you know, you'll be lying. I wouldn't be surprised if you told me now that Olofé wanted to go to bed with you and you with Olofé.

MAN: You don't know what you're saying. I only wanted what he had.

WOMAN: That makes no sense.

MAN: Yes, it does, because if I had what he had, then I could possess *you*.

WOMAN: *(Sighing.)* . . . what Olofé has . . . ! Who could have here *(She points to her genitals.)* what Olofé has! No, you don't understand, you can't understand. Who could . . . ? Because all this started long ago. Every night, even before you were born, Olofé was around. I've told you time and again . . . When you prayed at night . . . When you prayed to Olofé . . . *(Pause.)* You see, Olofé was your father . . .

MAN: Each prayer, each word, each letter, turned me against Olofé. You made me go to sleep with your chanting, but I could see him in my sleep just the same.

WOMAN: *(Laughing.)* Not now, Olofé! I have a headache, Olofé! Later, later, Olofé! Stop it, Olofé! My old man's going to catch us, Olofé! Go on! No, stop! Go on, go on, Olofé! Don't, don't leave now, Olofé! *(Looking at the man after the ecstasy she has experienced during her reminiscing.)* You can't possibly understand. You never have. No, not even you. No one can compare to Olofé. He was the greatest. And don't misunderstand me; I'm not trying to hurt your feelings.

MAN: *(Shaking her.)* Why don't you get this straight once and for all? I had the razor to cut off from Olofé what I needed to be like him, what you also wanted to have.

WOMAN: *(Laughing.)* Now? Heavens, no, Olofé! If we do it now the other Olofé in there will see us! Please, for baby Olofé's sake. He's watching us in the mirror . . . Right now? In front of him, I can't. Olofé, please, your son Olofé is staring at us. I'm so embarrassed, so ashamed! Olofé, please, don't take off my clothes in front of him.

MAN: *(Very violently, as if there were someone in the mirror.)* You son of a bitch!

WOMAN: Don't be angry, Olofé!

MAN: You, bitch!

WOMAN: *(The man shakes her violently, but this only excites her voluptuousness even more.)* Oh, yes, go on, hard, Olofé! Beat me, crush me!

MAN: Listen! Listen to me well! That night, when you thought I was asleep . . . *(He displays the razor as he begins to refer to it.)* It was sharp, ready to cut, and I had it hidden in me. I drew near to him and he thought I was you . . . The son of a bitch . . . ! He was lying in bed, with his legs widespread, like this . . . *(He pulls her by the hair in such a way that she ends up on top of him. His head is now falling from the bed, facing the audience.)* Do you understand now? You didn't notice a thing because when you came into the dark room I was already wearing what I had cut off Olofé.

WOMAN: You're wrong. I'm the one who's really Olofé. *(She raises an arm. She is holding the razor now. He still has her by the hair but since his head is hanging back, he cannot see her holding the open razor.)*

MAN: Once and for all, get it straight. I have what Olofé *used* to have. It's mine now. It's all mine. I am now, and always will be, Olofé's true son. Look between my legs. Isn't that what Olofé had? Don't you recognize it?

WOMAN: No, it's all mine, not yours. What you took from Olofé belongs only to me, and when I have it you won't be able to leave me ever again. It is I who'll have what Olofé had, for I am the earth and the sky! I have his sacred blade. *I am, forever, Olofé! (She lowers the razor and in a single blow castrates the man. As the man's scream is heard, the lights go out.)*

CURTAIN

Note

[1]*Oculé Mayá* is a popular version of the African phrase *Ocuelé Mayá*, possibly Yoruba in origin, used in religious chants. It means "Good afternoon, Goddess." In Cuba it is used to greet the goddess Yemanyá, Changó's mother, and it is equivalent to "Hail, Yemanyá."

Four Minidramas

The Meeting
Doll's Play
Declaration of Principles
A Flower Vendor for These Times

René Ariza

René Ariza

René Ariza was born in Havana in 1940. At the age of sixteen he entered Havana's Academy of Dramatic Arts, and a year later made his television debut as an actor in José Antonio Alonso's show. In 1958 he completed *Cántico*, his first collection of poems. Until 1967 he was involved as both actor and director with theater groups such as Teatro Estudio, Los Doce, and Grupo Ocuje, while still maintaining contacts with radio, television, and cinema. In 1967 his play, *La vuelta a la manzana*, received the UNEAC (Unión de Escritores y Artistas de Cuba) Prize. Another play, *El banquete*, received two nominations for the same prize a year later.

In 1971 Ariza was removed from his job for "not having the required ideological convictions." Three years later all of his written works were reviewed and confiscated, and he was sentenced to eight years in prison. Ariza was imprisoned "For writing short stories and essays whose contents and scope reveal a marked ideological diversion, and which are counterrevolutionary propaganda. These texts, of no artistic value, in addition, were sent abroad in order to discredit our Revolution and were an attempt against the Socialist Dogmas and the International Solidarity." Ariza continued writing in prison. As a result of international efforts, an amnesty for certain political prisoners gave him his freedom in 1979 and brought him to the United States. Upon his arrival in Miami, he gave a number of recitals and read some of his plays. He became very active as a painter, traveling often to San Francisco where he finally settled in 1983. While continuing his artistic endeavors, Ariza is also working on a theater project which takes special performances to jails, schools, parks, and homes for elderly people.

In his concise dramas, Ariza presents out of the ordinary aspects of human behavior as well as psychological conflicts. His plays, including the four found in this volume, contain well-calculated doses of humor and irony within the frame of what could be classified as theater of the absurd. For example, in *The Meeting* (1971), the man who is supposed to deliver a speech is unable to communicate his message. One might conjecture that the author is pointing out the futility of such gatherings. One could also see in the protagonist a deliberate effort to remain silent in order to avoid trouble. The second character, the one who is eager to become involved, agrees to the nonsense, perhaps because to disagree would mean being singled out as a disruptive element. *Doll's Play* (1971) reveals the cruelty often hidden behind motherly love. The situation is aggravated by the presence of a father of dubious morality who regularly beats his daughter while the mother verbally harasses her, calling her "dummy," "ugly," and "stupid." The girl ends up doing to her mother what she had promised to do to her doll for misbehaving. This is realized by way of an unexpected role reversal in which the characters experience a complex personality shift. Mother, daughter, and doll become, respectively, doll, daughter, and mother, with the girl taking final control of the situation. *Declaration of Principles* (1979) deals with a lascivious man who disguises his desires in an aura of self-righteousness. *A Flower Vendor for These Times* (1980) reveals another aspect of rare human behavior. In this work, the character, although wanting the beautiful things which life offers and which she cannot afford, trains herself to enjoy the decayed, the old, and the ruined. Her stoic acceptance brings her the resignation she needs to keep on living in the deepest misery. A mystery surrounds the play as the vendor prophesies a day when her order will rule us all.

The Meeting

Characters

MAN 1
MAN 2

Man 1 goes to the podium. Brief applause.

MAN 1: Ahem . . . Er . . . Well . . . *(Quick sigh.)* Ladies . . . and gentlemen . . . Ahem . . . Well . . . I mean, comrades . . . It's . . . Well . . . What I mean to say is . . . I've gathered you here . . . I mean . . . We've gathered here . . . So that I can tell you . . . That is . . . So that . . . To comment . . . on . . . In other words . . . *(Silence.)*

MAN 2: *(He raises his hand timidly amidst the embarrassing silence.)* I . . . would like . . . to say . . . something which . . .

MAN 1: *(Regaining control of the situation, very annoyed.)* Silence! *(Pause. He looks everyone present in the eyes.)* As I was saying when I was interrupted . . . Ahem . . . Well . . . What I mean to say is . . . We've gathered here . . . *(Silence. Man 2 appears restless.)* Since I . . . You see . . . Er . . . As I was saying . . . *(A long silence. Man 2 looks at everyone and then, shyly, raises his hand. Everyone looks at him.)*

MAN 2: I only wanted to . . .

MAN 1: Silence! So then . . . As I was saying at first . . . Er . . . Ahem . . . That I . . . Well . . . Since I . . . We . . . After all . . . Um . . . *(Silence. Everyone looks at Man 2 who shrinks back into his chair.)* In my opinion . . . Ahem . . . I . . . You know . . . and . . . *(A long silence. The people gathered there begin to show signs of impatience.)*

MAN 2: *(Very quickly.)* I just wanted to say . . .

MAN 1: SILENCE! *(He looks at Man 2 as if he were an intruder. With his eyes he commands all others to look at Man 2 in the same manner, which they do.)* I . . . Well . . . That is . . . After . . . What I mean to say . . . Er . . . Ahem . . . *(He clears his throat.)* What I . . . We . . . You know . . . and . . . *(Turns to Man 2.)* Silence! As I was saying . . . I . . . Hum . . . In my opinion . . . What I . . . That is . . . What . . . *(He speaks more rapidly and loudly as he breathes deeply.)* Ahem . . . Er . . . Um . . . Then . . . Ahem . . . And . . . Er . . . Uh! . . . *(He finally stops and slumps down. Prolonged, absolute silence. People show their impatience. He turns quickly to Man 2 and smiles.)* You have the floor now. *(The others look at him with relief.)*

MAN 2: *(Delighted.)* I am in total agreement with everything you've said. *(General confusion. Brief silence, followed by prolonged, loud applause.)*

CURTAIN

Doll's Play

Characters

THE GIRL
THE MOTHER

A girl carrying a large doll enters. Girl and doll resemble one another. They dress alike; they have the same bitter expression.

THE GIRL: *(Talking to the doll.)* You know what I'm gonna do with you if you don't eat your soup? I'm gonna put you back in your box, cover it with the lid, tie the box with the ribbon and let you rot in there until I'm a big girl. *(She sits center stage. "The Mother" enters wearing a night gown like the ones "The Girl" and the doll are wearing.)*

THE MOTHER: *(She has the same bitter expression.)* What are you doing up this late, you dummy?

THE GIRL: My girl doesn't want to go to school.

THE MOTHER: How can you be so stupid? Don't you realize that's nothing but a doll?

THE GIRL: Yes, but she's my daughter. Do you think I can just let her do as she pleases?

THE MOTHER: Go to bed right now if you don't want me to smash that ugly face of yours.

THE GIRL: I can't. First I have to do all the household chores. Then, I have her dress to iron and I have to make her breakfast. I'm fed up with her!

THE MOTHER: When your father gets home, drunk as always, you'll see. He'll really let you have it.

THE GIRL: Those are my exact words. *(Addressing the doll.)* When your father gets home, drunk as usual . . .

THE MOTHER: For God's sake!! Why, but why did I ever buy her that . . . damn doll?

THE GIRL: *(Addressing the doll.)* Why, but why did I have to be your mother? There are so many nice girls out there who don't have dolls . . . and who are so very happy!

THE MOTHER: You know what I'm gonna do to you? I'll give you an enema you'll remember for the rest of your life.

THE GIRL: *(Addressing the doll.)* You heard her, didn't you?

THE MOTHER: *(Sarcastic.)* I'm talking to you, you idiot; I'm talking to you and not to your stupid doll.

THE GIRL: *(Addressing the doll.)* I'm talking to you, you idiot.

THE MOTHER: When your father gets home, after doing whatever it is that he does out there, I'm gonna tell him all about you. He always has enough energy left to take off his belt and whip you real good . . . and you know he'll do it.

THE GIRL: *(Talking to "The Mother.")* You know, yesterday he had to give her an injection. This cutie pie didn't want to go to bed.

THE MOTHER: *(Pause. Confused.)* That's exactly what he had to do. How permissive can one be?

THE GIRL: *(In total complicity with "The Mother.")* I know he has others . . . Marianita, who lives down the street, has a Barbie by him, and with Conchita he had a Raggedy Ann. But with me it's a whole different story: he has to behave like a real father.

THE MOTHER: You're doing the right thing. Look at me, and listen to what I have to say. *(She twists her face and keeps this gesture for a few seconds. Pause.)* You know what I'd do in your shoes? I'd make her do all the household chores while I took it easy.

THE GIRL: But, mommy, don't you see she's just a doll?

THE MOTHER: *(Confused.)* What? She's just . . . ?

THE GIRL: Rudy, Rosaura's little Rudy is the father.

THE MOTHER: How could you let Rudy do that to you?

THE GIRL: Oh, well . . . ! Would you believe one day Rudy wanted to operate on her and get all of her stuffing out to punish her . . . ? But I didn't let him: don't forget she's my daughter.

THE MOTHER: Sure! But things won't be the same around here anymore. Just wait until that dirty father of yours gets home. You'll see.

THE GIRL: Don't count on it. I have a confession to make. Yesterday when he started to hit me I neither cried nor screamed, remember? And it was all because I knew all along that I was my doll and not me.

THE MOTHER: *(Pointing to the doll.)* But how could you let her do that to you? Can't you see that that . . . *monster* is playing tricks on you and changing places with you?

THE GIRL: I know. But motherly love is a wonderful thing. *(Pause. She looks at "The Mother.")* And I love you so, my child . . . *("The Mother" has acquired a doll-like stiffness. The girl treats her from now on as she treated her doll before.)* Didn't I tell you to eat your soup? *("The Mother" does not answer.)* And go to bed right now. When your father gets home, drunk as usual, he's gonna whip you with his belt. *("The Mother" is now sitting on the floor. "The Girl" addresses the doll.)* Mother, what's wrong with you? You look like a . . . *("The Girl" laughs.)* like a doll. *(Addressing "The Mother.")* And you . . .You don't wanna go to school, nor eat your soup, nor go to bed. I'm not gonna keep repeating myself; I'm sick and tired of it. This very instant . . . *("The Girl" leaves the stage and returns with an oversize box.)* I'm gonna put you in your box . . . *(She gets "The Mother" inside the box with some difficulty and then addresses the doll.)* Why did you have to buy me such a big doll? *("The Girl" closes the box or puts the lid on it and then ties a ribbon around it. She then talks to the doll.)* I don't want her anymore, Mommy. *(Talking to the closed box.)* You'll stay there until I'm a big girl. *(Talking to the doll.)* Mother, you look tired. Come, I'll take you to bed. *(She takes the doll and leaves singing.)* "Mary had a little lamb, little lamb, little lamb. Mary had a little lamb . . . *(The box, tied with the ribbon, remains on stage.)*

Declaration of Principles

At stage rear, a man looks out of a window he has just opened. Several mirrors will reflect his image from different angles throughout this work. He speaks to the audience, surprised at what he sees.

MAN: Two men hugging and kissing! That's filthy, indecent! They say that's love . . . To me, that's . . . I don't know. Have no idea. They're shameless. Listen, the important thing is to keep one's decorum. Otherwise, you fall, and if you do . . . You know what I mean. It's unbelievable! If I weren't seeing it with my own eyes . . . It's such a . . . *(Disgusted)* If a guy like one of those two ever tries something fishy with me, I'll . . . *(He punches the air and laughs, jokingly.)* Well, at least he would have to pay me a pretty penny . . . buy me a mansion . . . *(He becomes serious.)* with a swimming pool Hollywood style, and green hills around, and horses . . . And a nice chick before anything else. *(He looks out again.)* But just look at them! What do you think? And you? How about you? *(Nervous.)* Why don't you tell me what you really think? *(Addressing the audience.)* Yet there are people who enjoy watching something like that. They're just as shameful as those who do it, . . . because in the end . . . *(He looks out the window.)* If they had at least gone to one of those bars . . . it'd be a different matter. It's not that I condone it, but . . . *(He looks out.)* but that's a joke. *(Speaking in a confidential tone.)* It's really dirty, I tell you. *(He stares in silence. Turning to the audience.)* Ladies and gentlemen, I think, *(He checks his watch.)* that those two have nothing else to do . . . They're not only filthy, but a couple of bums to boot. They don't want to contribute to this society . . . or any other one! To produce, to be useful, to work . . . that's what they're paid for. *(He talks lost in thought. As in a dream, his face contracts.)* They get paid so that they can buy what they need to live: clothes, food, a car, furniture, a home, a watch, jewelry, mirrors, paintings, amusement, cigarettes, magazines, newspapers, drinks, cocaine . . . *(Lost in thought.)* and all the necessities . . . But they don't! They are . . . *(He spits.)* mere pigs who go against the system, against *the truth of life. (He looks out.)* As if they really loved one another. *(Passionately.)* And they don't. I swear they don't! That's why they should be crushed and boiling water poured between their legs. You know what I'd do? I'd smash their . . . and stick pins in their arms, and put zippers on their . . . *(He makes the sign of the cross.)* They'd have to suffer! It's the only way, don't you see? Do you get my point, sir? Do you, lady? *(He changes his mood. He looks out, surprised at what he sees.)* What? I can't believe it! They've changed . . . They're not . . . men. No! I made a mistake. Must have been the light. *(Absent-minded.)* Forgive me. *(He blesses himself and then looks out the window.)* But, what are they? They're two broads . . . and great looking too! This is getting better. TWO WOMEN! Great! *(He rubs his hands with delight as he looks out the window. Noticing the audience, he apologizes.)* Yes . . . well, once in a while, I like to watch . . . things like this. What I mean is . . . don't get me wrong . . . I'm not into this kind of action, but . . . Well, I'm not like them. The truth is that what they're doing is as wrong as what I thought the two guys were doing. It's a shame, just the same. It's . . . *(He searches for the right words.)* against nature, like when I thought at first they were two fags. *(He changes his tone.)* But once in a blue moon, you know, I enjoy . . . *(He looks at the audience as though they were all in it together and then looks out the window.)* What a sight! *(Confessing to the audience.)* I have some films in . . . a drawer . . . ! And quite a collection of magazines and pictures. They have all kinds of . . . *(He changes his tone rapidly.)* It's all indecent, filthy, and that's the truth. *(He addresses an old man in the audience.)* Garbage! . . . And yet, it helps, you know, when one no longer can . . . Do you follow me? *(Distant, anguished.)* Sometimes when . . . You know what I mean, don't you sir? *(He speaks like a teacher.)* I think that, to a certain extent, those magazines, and all those porno gadgets—vibrators, plastic things, dolls, books, artificial genitals—fulfill a social need. *(He changes his tone.)* Not me, of course. All that really makes me sick. But if anyone wants to use that junk, it's O.K. with me. It's really none of my business. I'm me. *(Anguished.)* I'm myself. *(He looks out the window and changes his tone.)* Wow, how those two enjoy one another! There, that's it! *(He mimicks a boxing match, punching the air and whispering words of encouragement to the fighters.)* There, grab her! Get on her! *(More aggressively.)* Your turn, now. Go ahead. Let her have it! *(He looks at the audience, smiling.)* This is great. *(He looks again, then takes a few steps back in astonishment.)* What? Oh, I can't believe this! I know one of those two. *(He is terrified at his new finding.)* It can't be! *(He tries to hide his growing anguish from the audience. He preens in front of the mirrors, as he composes himself. As he speaks, he emphasizes his words.)* I don't look too bad, do I? Yes, I've lost a little more hair this summer, but not that much . . . *(He combs his hair.)* but I can still pass for thirty . . . *(He cannot suppress his anguish. He tries not to look out the window, but an irresistible impulse makes him do so. Then he turns to the audience. When he now speaks, his tone will be between lordly and pathetic.)* Sometimes one has bitter experiences in life. One . . . after a lifetime of sacrifices, hardships, hopes, and dreams, sees things that make one doubt even his own family. *(He looks again. Mumbling words of anguish, he whispers.)* It's so horrible . . . *(He changes his tone.)* NO . . . *(Suddenly, he smiles.)* But it isn't . . . It isn't! How could I ever think . . . It was all a trick the light played on me! How deceiving things seem in the wrong light! *(He kneels down and then addresses the audience.)* Forgive me, mother! How could I believe for one instant that such a filthy act . . . *(He looks out the window again and changes his tone.)* They're putting on a real show. *(He laughs.)* They're too much. *(Speaking in a lascivious tone.)* Go on, go on! That's the way to do it! Go on, baby! *(He twists his body exaggeratedly in pleasure, his back to the audience. All of a sudden he realizes what is really happening outside. Pause. Still turned away from the audience, he straightens up, amazed at the sight before him.)* I can't believe this! This is so wild! The light keeps playing tricks on me. Another mistake! Damn! *(He changes his tone deceptively.)* They're just a man and a woman. Big deal! *(He chuckles to himself.)* What a joke! And I thought all along . . . *(He pays no attention to what is happening outside.)* But the fact is, I don't really understand *those* women . . . Two guys I can understand . . . if you're really horny, or you're in jail, or in the army, or there's no other way . . . But two . . . two women . . . There's nothing they can do with one another. It's crazy! They have nothing with which to penetrate . . . and that . . . that's what sex is all about . . . and I'll say it and say it again. *(Lost in thought.)* It's the only way in which I . . . *(He whispers.)* Even if . . . *(He smiles.)* But no. As you can see, I made another mistake. Lights can fool you. *(Always talking to the audience.)* Bah! Nothing but a man and a woman. Such a normal thing! Nothing unusual about that. *(He prances before the mirrors, looking at himself and trying to straighten himself up. He pulls in his stomach, fixes his hair, and corrects his posture as he speaks calmly.)* Although . . . I've no idea why they have to do it out there, that way . . . After all . . . sex is a private matter. When a guy's with a woman, he shouldn't . . . he shouldn't do certain things . . . It's all a matter of . . . *(He looks at himself.)* I still look O.K. Yet . . . I'll have to *(He combs his hair so as to cover his bald spot. He picks up his train of thought again.)* Nowadays there are so many things you can do to hide your age. *(He touches up his moustache with a brush.)* It's not that I find this unnatural . . . It isn't . . . but you owe some respect to others. *(He prances in front of the mirror, watching his mannequin-like posture.)* And that respect for others is what makes us different from animals . . . don't you know? Carrying on like that in public is shameless. *(He rearranges the position of his penis so that it becomes more noticeable.)* Decorum is the norm, and what is the norm is moral, and morality is something su . . . su . . . sublime quite often, because God *(Speaking as in a trance.)*, God Almighty teaches us what is right, that is . . . *(He combs his hair repeatedly.)* like immaculate clouds, or the flight of birds, signs of the purest and most sacred of states. *(Suddenly he decides to look out the window again. Before doing so, with a gesture he requests permission of the audience.)* If at least they didn't do it . . . out in the open, and with such pleasure . . . If, at least, instead of doing that filth . . . *(Turning abruptly to the audience.)* Because it is indecent, depending on how you do it. *(He looks again, lost in thought.)* If they only wore chains and hurt each other . . . If he'd only hit her. Or if he'd let her hit his buns real hard . . . or let her slap him and hit him all over . . . *(Facing the audience, he pantomimes a masochistic sexual act.)* There! Punch hard! Keep on punching! That's it! Don't stop! Now bite me, baby! Go on, make me bleed!

Yeah! *(With pain on his face and in his voice.)* Wow, that was something else! *(He recovers. Now on his knees, he speaks to the audience.)* That's the only way to get a kick out of sex. Don't you agree, sir? Don't you? And if one gets real pleasure out of something, one must pay the price. That's the law of supply and demand . . . you know. If one enjoys something like that which isn't . . . which is . . . which isn't . . . That's God's law enacted by men on this earth, and that's the way it is, period. *(He looks again.)* My, . . . but . . . it seems as if they . . . as if they were having more fun than . . . I can't understand how they can be so wild . . . If at least she were wearing stockings and a necklace . . . and he were wearing shoes and a watch . . . In that case, perhaps . . . But they haven't placed a mirror anywhere to watch themselves "in action" . . . How strange, how very strange. They aren't sniffing anything either. All they do is embrace each other. How silly . . . What a waste of time . . . I want *no part* of that nonsense . . . I haven't lost what it takes yet . . . CREEPS! *(He slams the window shut and walks off stage like a priest in a hurry.)*

CURTAIN

A Flower Vendor for These Times

A woman carrying a basket of dead flowers crosses the stage. She wears an old and wrinkled evening gown.

WOMAN: *(She cries out in a sweet voice.)* Withered flowers! Withered flowers! Would you care to buy some flowers, sir? *(Speaking to herself.)* I can't understand why people don't like withered flowers. I just can't understand it. What difference does it make? You buy freshly cut flowers and they just die anyway. *(She looks at a flower stand with freshly cut flowers nearby.)* Look at those prices . . . The chrysanthemums cost . . . Isn't that something? I know you can't pay that price. On the other hand, my merchandise is the cheapest around. You'll never find flowers as cheap as mine. Trust me. I don't know why ladies don't like to pin on a corsage of dead gardenias, and no gentleman pins on his lapel a carnation that has begun to turn black. *(Addressing the audience in a confidential tone.)* The people with bad taste that one has to put up with! . . . The fact is that they just don't understand things as they really are. Yes . . . At first I even thought I was crazy. Now I know better. It took a while for me to get all this straight, but now . . . Everything I use or wear is old and worn. I'm not stupid. The other day . . . I was hungry . . . Well . . . I was! I went to a fruit store. The apples cost a fortune, and the pears and bananas were sky-high. My stomach was making all kinds of noises. I kept staring and staring at the fruit, but to no avail. My looking didn't make my hunger go away. I talked to the owner of the shop and explained my situation to him. He said he couldn't care less, and that my hunger was no concern of his. I knew he was right. After all, what could he do? But I knew better, so . . . I waited and waited several days. I was famished . . . but I kept my cool. As the fruit got riper, the owner gradually reduced the price. The time finally came when it could be bought for practically nothing. The man kept on looking at his fruit in despair. The fruit was rotting, but no one was buying it. Then he finally gave it to me . . . in a manner of speaking, because he actually took in payment the sticky quarter I had been turning in my hand all the while I waited. *(She sighs.)* Oh, well . . . if I hadn't been patient . . . I wouldn't have gotten them at such a bargain.

Withered flowers, ma'am? Wanna buy some flowers, young lady? *(Continuing.)* You know, I've gotten used to it. I buy nothing fresh. What am I gonna buy it with? Why do you look at me with such disgust? Once you get used to it, you won't even notice you're eating rotten fruit. The same goes for flowers. *(She cries out.)* Withered flowers! You see my dress? When it was in fashion it cost a fortune. I got it for nothing. A lady I know called to me as I was passing by selling flowers, and offered it to me. She no longer wanted it, but I did. *(Sincerely.)* She's very good-hearted. Whenever she doesn't want something, she donates it to me or to someone else. She gave a friend of mine a refrigerator. It's true it was broken, but how could my friend even dream of having a refrigerator, broken or not? The lady told her all she had to do was take it away from her yard. *(Pause as she reflects on the matter.)* I think that in the end it was useless, but it's the thought that counts, isn't it? It was outside for two weeks while my friend and her husband dragged it home, step by step . . . Of course it rained on it several times. *(Lowering her voice.)* It was no good when she gave it to them . . . but by the time they got it home, it was totally ruined. But it looked great. And the same thing happens with flowers. If you can't afford them fresh, buy them dead. In the end you'll learn to enjoy them just the same.

Withered flowers! Would you like to buy some wilted flowers, young man? They're the best gift you could get your fiancée. They're real cheap. You just can't get anything better for the price. Let me tell you a true story. It happened to me. One day, when I was young, I saw this bunch of beautiful red roses in the window of a very expensive shop in my neighborhood. I kept admiring them. They were so perfect they didn't even look real. I couldn't dream of buying them, even in those days when things were relatively cheap. Well, in the end, a young man passed by with his fiancée, a girl I had seen in the neighborhood, and he bought the flowers for her. He was rich, of course, and he gave her the roses to win her heart. *(Lowering her voice.)* Although now, flowers have gone up in price so much! Oh well, that's the way things are, and that's that. They just cost more, much more. A mum will cost you an arm and a leg, and a freshly cut one . . . whatever they ask for it. So you'll make a better deal getting my withered chrysanthemums. They're great, and you can get them real cheap. Besides, they'll never look worse than they do now. They'll stay just the same—dried up. Believe me, I never put flowers that aren't dead in my own house. No one is going to make me change now. I know what I like. Besides, . . . that's all I can afford. The young man I was telling you about bought his fiancée the red roses, and a few days later the flowers were a real eyesore. So, why not buy my roses that are already shriveled? My dead roses are . . . *(She searches for an adjective that would describe them exactly, then addresses a man.)* Listen, nowadays the price of a bunch of roses like those in my story . . . well, they're out of the question. I don't think you could buy them even if you gave all you have for them . . . even your own body. They're for the very rich—the duchesses, the real ladies, the women like those you see in the movies or read about in magazines or novels. Oh God! That's great! That's the life! *(She changes mood.)* But I don't live in a world of dreams, no sir. Old things are all I need. Follow my example . . . you won't regret it. Faded flowers! Would you care to buy some faded flowers?

Let me give you another example. When I was young, I was beautiful, . . . a real cutie. I met a young man who . . . heavens! . . . was driving me wild. He was a real hunk. I wanted him so bad that I was going insane. I followed him everywhere. I tried every trick in the book to get his attention, but nothing worked . . . He never even looked at me. As if I didn't exist. And then . . . well, time passed by. I kept working on him, and he kept ignoring me. Finally I resigned myself to living without him, the same resignation I now have about everything. I said to myself, "No way I'm going to ruin my life on account of him. Now he doesn't have the time of day for me. But let time pass . . . you'll see . . ." And I waited. I waited more than twenty years, no, thirty years. *(Pause.)* Well, when he was old, fat, wrinkled, gray, and practically bald, his nose twisted by the ravages of time, and a cute birthmark on his cheek had become a disgusting dark wart . . . then, he finally came to me. His last wife had died, and he came and proposed. He is now my husband, the beautiful man I had always wanted. True, he looks horrible today, but isn't he the same man I dreamed about? It's all in your mind. Who won in the end? Didn't I get him after all? Isn't that what counts? I was patient and I caught him. That's why I don't want handsome young men. I want them old and bald, with potbellies. I've grown used to the idea. That has been my philosophy of life for quite a while now. But people have individual tastes, and one must respect them. *(Showing her merchandise.)* Withered flowers, sir! Faded flowers, young lady! *(Lowering her voice.)* No one's buying anything from me . . . I can't imagine what they think. *(Continuing.)* To tell you the truth, the night he came to propose I didn't recognize him. It took him over half an hour to refresh my memory. Only by making an effort could I tell the old man was the same handsome guy who had driven me crazy.

Dead flowers, ma'am! Shriveled flowers for your wife, sir! How can people be so foolish? It's so simple! They don't realize that dead flowers are a thousand times better than freshly cut ones. They're so cheap, and fresh ones are so darn costly. The same goes for people. Beautiful people cost too much! If you, sir, invite a beautiful woman out to dinner, watch out . . . you'll spend a fortune. And not only that, you'll have to wear your most expensive suit, a nice cologne, good shoes . . . Your car can't be an old jalopy; it has to look right. And then you have to empty your wallet in elegant bars, restaurants, fashionable places . . . not to mention the presents she'll expect from you. I'm telling you, to get a beautiful lady you'll have to pay through the nose. And a love affair like those in romance novels will cost a bundle . . . *(Pause.)* That's O.K. for the rich, but I don't kid myself. I'll do just fine with old withered flowers and potbellied old men. *(Gently.)* Faded flowers for sale! Look, if anyone takes a shine to me, he won't have to spend much. I'm neither young nor pretty, that's why I won't cost as much as the others. That's the way it ought to be. Withered flowers! They aren't in much demand around here . . . But there's no reason to despair. I know they'll want my flowers real soon . . . and all of them will ask for withered flowers instead of fresh ones, and they'll all want potbellied men instead of handsome guys. I'm just counting the minutes until that day comes . . . Meanwhile I'll just keep selling my flowers. Faded flowers! Dead flowers! Listen, freshly cut flowers are so expensive . . . so expensive that you can't even afford to look at them. *(Naively.)* And I wonder, why do chrysanthemums and roses have to be sold at all? *(She looks at the audience.)* Because they're part of nature, aren't they? *(She changes her mood.)* I'm no fool. I know my limits. You can get a kick out of old things too if you know how. *(She cries out.)* Wilted flowers! Dead flowers! *(She sighs.)* Good God, nowadays no one wants to buy them! *(She smiles.)* But soon, very soon . . . they'll want nothing else. You'll see! The fresh flowers will be so darn expensive that only millionaires, high ranking military officers, and ladies wrapped in expensive coats will be able to buy them. One can see that coming. Withered flowers, sir! Withered flowers, miss! *(She sighs.)* Oh . . . life, life! Just look at that. Two young women passed by just now. Were they ever beautiful! They looked like me . . . in the good old days. But just look at me now. You know why I look this way? Because of the hard times I've lived through. But no more. No sir. I suffered because I wanted to have what I couldn't have. How could anyone hope for good things like . . . eating every day, being loved, having a decent roof over one's head? Those are luxuries that only the rich and powerful can afford. I know that perfectly well. I know my place. Now I'm content with pudgy old men, living in a hut, and selling withered flowers . . . even if no one buys them. Dead flowers, sir! Faded flowers, ma'am! You may not buy them today, but one day you will. I know that sooner than you think, you'll buy them . . . Withered flowers . . . ! *(She walks away, hawking her wares.)*

CURTAIN

The Great American Justice Game

Miguel González-Pando

Miguel González-Pando

Although Miguel González-Pando was born in Cienfuegos, province of Las Villas, in 1941, he spent his childhood and adolescence in Havana. In March 1958 his political involvement against the Batista regime forced him to leave his homeland, and he went to Washington, D.C., where his exile lasted only a few months. Political amnesty, granted to those who had abandoned their country, allowed him to return to Cuba in October of the same year.

At the end of 1960, González-Pando left Cuba again only to return in April 1961 with the forces of the ill-fated invasion of the Bay of Pigs. The failure of this effort resulted in his capture, and he was sentenced to a thirty-year prison term. As part of a settlement between Cuba and the United States, González-Pando and a number of prisoners taken by the Cuban government during the invasion were returned to the United States on Christmas Day 1962 in exchange for medicine and humanitarian supplies. González-Pando settled in Miami where he earned a Bachelor's degree in Business Administration (1966) from the University of Miami. From 1966 to 1969, he was a graduate student in the Department of Economics at Harvard University. Since 1970 he has lived in Miami, where he has taken an active part in political, educational, and civil rights issues related to Hispanics. In 1973 he joined the faculty at Florida International University. At present, he serves as Director of Latino Studies at that institution.

To date, González-Pando has written two full-length plays which reflect his concern with the minority experience in America. *La familia Pilón*, written in Spanish in 1981, was staged in Miami by Bilingual/Bicultural Productions that same year. The play is a comedy-drama relating the struggles of a Cuban family in coping with the social pressures of acculturation. *The Great American Justice Game*, which we include here in an abridged adaptation prepared by the author especially for this volume, was written originally in English and completed in 1987. The play is a hard-hitting satire which underscores the cultural castration suffered by those who fail to meet the requirements of mainstream American society. The author says about his work: "What would happen if present efforts to make English the official language of the United States, carried to the extreme, were to culminate in the passage of a law forbidding the use of other languages? Such is the absurd premise of the play." The action, set in the year 2005, centers on María Libertad, who remains silent until the very end of the farce. She is brought to trial for having violated the fictive English and English Only Act by using Spanish. This is the only language she has been taught by her parents who fled to avoid giving up their mother tongue. The trial, in the fashion of a television game show, will decide the nature of María Libertad's punishment. The play, full of irony and humorous situations, denounces the intolerance of those conservatives in American society who disregard the basic principles upon which this nation was built. González-Pando's voice is one that speaks loud and clear, from his very personal perspective, in the name of all minority groups.

The Great American Justice Game

From "Them," with Hope

My first thought was to call it "The Day the American Dream Became a Nightmare." Fortunately, I dismissed that impulse—not so much because it sounded pedantic, but because such a long title would appear cramped on the theater marquee.

The story is based upon a dream that my daughter once had. It is true that the American dream has often eluded large segments of our society, hence the polarization between the "us" and the "them." To "them"—the Black, the Indian, the Jew, the Hispanic, and all who simply do not appear to conform to the requirements of the mainstream culture as defined by "us"—the existential struggle lies just one step away from turning into a nightmare.

María Libertad is one of "them," and the fictional passage of the English and English Only Act of 1990 represents the step that turns her life into a nightmare. Whether the premise of this play ever becomes a reality may be debatable. Suffice it to say that our history has witnessed worse examples of cultural castration.

The play, above all, attempts to entertain. It also attempts to be historically correct—allowing, of course, for a degree of dramatic license. As the history buff will soon discover, the events bearing upon the play have actually taken place, and even major portions of the text spoken by the characters have been adapted from authentic sources. If this personal vision of our society is presented in a manner that causes both amusement and embarrassment to the audience's sensitivities, I have then fulfilled my hope of reaching into its consciousness to shake with laughter the comfortable rationalizations that have served "us" all too well.

Miguel González-Pando
January 1987

Characters

LIBERTY, voluptuous Latin woman in a Statue of Liberty costume. She represents the conscience of America. She speaks only to the audience, as the other characters can neither see nor hear her.

JUDGE, gay man with Spanish accent and exaggerated mannerisms, wearing heavy makeup. He doubles as judge in the trial and host of the game show, speaking through a megaphone, and switching from mocking pomposity to outright irreverence.

BAILIFF, fat man with German accent who affects childish attitudes. He represents the simpleminded fanatic.

MARIA, pretty fifteen-year-old girl with blonde hair and blue eyes. Defendant in the trial. She represents the victims of the supra-ethnic American nation as well as its hope for the future.

DEFENSE, articulate old man of weak character, concerned with formal legal procedures rather than justice. He represents the established order.

PROSECUTOR, passionate man with a strong personality. He represents bigotry.

CHORUS, composed of at least eight to ten actors, representing the mindless masses whose role in society is confined to being an echo. In a small production, the chorus may also be played by the celebrity witnesses, in which case they will move around the stage, but remain in semi-darkness until called upon individually to testify.

CELEBRITY WITNESSES, Founding Father, Noble Savage, Uncle Tom, White Supremacist, and Superman.

The action takes place circa 2005.

SCENE 1

The stage is dark. A dim light begins to shine over a voluptuous woman dressed as the Statue of Liberty. The light grows more intense as she speaks in a heavy Spanish accent. Chorus humming "America the Beautiful" in the background.

LIBERTY: *(Exaggeratedly sensual and seductive.)*
"Give me your tired, your poor,
Your huddled masses yearning to breathe free,
The wretched refuse of your teeming shore.
Send these, the homeless, tempest-tost to me,
I light my lamp beside the golden door."—
You know?

The music slowly gets out of tune, quick blackout.

JUDGE: Show time, show time, ladies and gentlemen, come in please! Show time, show time! What? Yes, the girls are inspected, but don't drink the water! Ha ha ha . . .

BAILIFF: *(Blowing a whistle.)* Silence! Silence! Hear ye, hear ye, this court is now in session. Honorable Fair N. Square presiding. And now, here comes the judge!

Curtains open. Set looks like that of a typical game show. From left to right: seating for the defense attorney, the defendant, the judge, the witness, the bailiff, and the prosecutor.

CHORUS: *(While Judge puts on his robe.)*
"Here comes the judge, here comes the judge,
clap your hands and rise to your feet
'cause he's Fair N. Square and he's got that beat.
Here comes the judge, here comes the judge,
clap your hands and rise to your feet
justice's coming with all deliberate speed."

JUDGE: Thank you, thank you, Bailiff. *(To the audience.)* Are you ready to play "The Great American Justice Game"? *(Using the megaphone.)* Bailiff, will you introduce today's contestants?

BAILIFF: The first contestant, representing the defense, is a full-blooded American, and his favorite pastime is watching old Perry Mason movies. And, our second contestant, representing the prosecution, can trace his ancestry all the way back to the Mayflower.

JUDGE: Let's give a fine round of applause to both of these one hundred percent Americans who will decide the fate of today's defendant in "The Great American Justice Game." And now, let's get ready to play! *(Suddenly turning pompous.)* Bring the defendant in! *(María Libertad, gagged, is brought in.)* Will the Bailiff read the charges!

BAILIFF: The defendant, María Libertad, is charged with the use of a foreign language in public, in violation of the English and English Only Act, which prescribes that English and English only shall be spoken in these United States. The defendant has continued to speak Spanish since she was found alone hiding in a cave deep within the Rocky Mountains. Furthermore, she has ignored all attempts to communicate with her in English.

JUDGE: *(Using the megaphone.)* And how does the defendant plead?

DEFENSE: I am entering a plea of nolo contendere . . .

BAILIFF: *(Blowing the whistle.)* English! English only!

CHORUS: English! English only!

DEFENSE: I am sorry, Your Honor; I mean "no contest." We plead no contest because the defendant never had an opportunity to learn English. She was born in the cave where her parents went into hiding when the English and English Only Act became law. Her parents, Your Honor, joined the massive exodus of Spanish speakers who decided to go underground rather than give up their language, and they taught her only Spanish.

PROSECUTOR: Your Honor, will you remind the defense that ignorance of the English language does not justify the use of any other language.

JUDGE: Five points under the category of "Put up or shut up" for the contestant for the prosecution, who takes an early lead! *(Using the megaphone.)* The defense is so reminded.

DEFENSE: I am not trying to justify anything, Your Honor—just explaining the facts: that the defendant, never having been taught English, could not help but speak Spanish.

PROSECUTOR: And how has the attorney for the defense come to know those facts? Did he communicate in Spanish with the defendant, Miss Libertad—or did she draw him a picture?

JUDGE: Five more points for the contestant for the prosecution under the category of "A picture is not worth a single English word"! The contestant for the prosecution now leads by ten points!

DEFENSE: Me use Spanish! Of course not! Being a law-abiding citizen, I have been careful not to discuss this case with the defendant. In fact, when I met María Libertad at the English and English Only Enforcement Agency, I asked the guards to gag her, and even then, as an additional precaution, I wore earmuffs, just in case . . . I can assure you, Your Honor, that no communication whatsoever has been established between the defendant and myself.

JUDGE: Those extreme precautions are worth ten points to the contestant for the defense under the category of "Covering your behind so your ass won't show"! And so, with the score even at ten points, we now have a tie game!

LIBERTY: This is a mockery of justice! A circus! You know? Is this what you call due process?

JUDGE: Since the contestant for the defense entered the plea of no contest, we will not be concerned with determining whether María Libertad is innocent or guilty. The question here is what would be an appropriate sentence—if she is found guilty, as certainly appears to be the case. Therefore, I want both contestants to address the issue of punishment in their opening statements.

PROSECUTOR: Your Honor, the English and English Only Act is clear and unequivocal: the defendant's insistence upon using Spanish, whether by choice or necessity, makes her guilty, and the sentence dictated by the law is her sterilization and commitment for life to a permanent detention center for hardcore speakers of foreign languages. There she shall remain isolated from society in order to ensure that her language and her ways do not contaminate this great nation of ours.

BAILIFF: Sterilize her! Sterilize her! *(Blowing the whistle.)* Let me do it!

CHORUS: Sterilize her! Sterilize her!

DEFENSE: Your Honor, María Libertad is merely a teenager. She needs to be rehabilitated, to be taught English. She can be naturalized and Americanized—it's still not too late for her.

LIBERTY: How can we discuss punishment before determining if the defendant is guilty or innocent, damn it! Besides, the defendant must be presumed innocent until proven guilty! María Libertad has the right to a fair trial, you know?

PROSECUTOR: Your Honor, the prosecution is prepared to introduce evidence showing that María Libertad is too old to undergo naturalization and Americanization. She will always remain a threat to our society unless she is sterilized and committed to the isolated environment of a permanent detention center.

BAILIFF: Sterilize her and cut her tongue off!

CHORUS: Sterilize her and cut her tongue off!

PROSECUTOR: I have here the record of thousands of documented cases of Spanish-speaking adolescents who were given the opportunity to participate in rehabilitation programs to become naturalized and Americanized. They did, of course, learn English, but consistently refused to forget their native language. At best, Your Honor, the defendant may become bilingual—and bilingualism is an even greater threat!

CHORUS: Bilingualism is an even greater threat!

JUDGE: That argument is worth five more points under the category of "You can't teach an old bitch new tricks." The contestant for the prosecution has again retaken a five-point lead!

PROSECUTOR: Thank you, Your Honor. I insist that María Libertad poses a serious threat to our society. Even if she could master the English language, we are responsible for ensuring that she would not teach Spanish secretly to others—to her children, for example. The law is clear, Your Honor: the defendant must be sterilized and remain isolated for the rest of her wretched life.

BAILIFF: Sterilize her! Sterilize her!

CHORUS: Sterilize her! Sterilize her!

PROSECUTOR: Need I remind this court how obstinate and sneaky these people are . . . the stubbornness with which they cling to their language and their ways? Just look how they reacted to the passage of the English and English Only Act: the very fact that millions of Spanish speakers deserted their jobs and abandoned their homes to take their families into hiding shows how dangerous these people can be.

JUDGE: Good! Five more points to the contestant for the prosecution under the category of "An ounce of sterility drugs is worth a ton of Spanish fly"! The contestant for the prosecution now leads the game by ten points.

DEFENSE: Your Honor, "these people" are not on trial—María Libertad is the only one on trial here! This girl cannot be tried as the reincarnation of those inferior "Frito Banditos" who under the guise of cultural pluralism once threatened to change America. Just look at her, Your Honor; does she seem dangerous to you? She even looks American—the girl is blonde and has blue eyes, for God's sake, your Honor!

JUDGE: I'm going to award ten full points to the contestant for the defense under the category of "Wrapping yourself with the American flag"! We again have a tie game! *(A loud horn blows.)* Oops! Do you know what that horn means? It means that now, the other contestant has only six seconds to blow the "horn of justice" and send this game into overtime! Bailiff, hand the horn of justice to the contestant for the prosecution and start counting!

BAILIFF: *(Chorus repeats each number.)* Six . . . five . . . four . . . three . . . two . . . one . . . *(Prosecutor blows the horn.)*

JUDGE: Good! With one second left the contestant for the prosecution beat the clock! Well, do you have a good counterargument to the "Wrap yourself with the American flag" appeal used by the contestant for the defense?

PROSECUTOR: I certainly do. Since the defense has appealed to our pride in America, Your Honor, I will call as my first celebrity witness none other than Mr. Founding Father himself.

JUDGE: That's a tremendous move by the contestant for the prosecution, sending the game into overtime! So, with the score even at twenty points, it will be his turn next to question the celebrity witness—but first, let's hear a word or two from our commercial sponsors, the people who make all this possible. Don't go away, 'cause we'll be right back to continue playing "The Great American Justice Game"! Studio audience, watch that monitor . . .

Black out and cut to pre-taped TV commercial.

COMMERCIAL *(Like in the Rolaids commercial.)*

REPORTER: We are now standing on the steps of the United Nations. They have just concluded a lengthy session, and we'll try to catch the American ambassador as he gets ready to leave. *(Looks around.)* Here comes Ambassador Hayakawa, the former senator from the state of California—let's see if he wants to say a few words. *(Calling Ambassador Hayakawa.)* Ambassador! Ambassador Hayakawa! *(Ambassador Hayakawa walks over.)* Ambassador, how do you spell "relief"?

AMBASSADOR: E-n-g-l-i-s-h: English! That's how I spell "relief . . . "

REPORTER: That's right folks, nothing takes the edge off a rough day of listening to the constant chatter of loud Spanish better than the soft and soothing sound of English. So . . . when you've had a long day full of "oye," "mira," "qué pasa," and "hola," come back to the only language that full-blooded Americans understand: English!

AMBASSADOR: E-n-g-l-i-s-h: English! That's how I spell "relief . . . "

VOICE OVER: English, void where prohibited by practice: places like the United Nations and most foreign countries.

SCENE 2

JUDGE: Welcome back to "The Great American Justice Game"! Our score is tied at twenty points apiece. And now, let's continue playing. *(Using the megaphone.)* If the contestant for the prosecution is ready, we'll call his first celebrity witness.

BAILIFF: *(Blowing the whistle.)* Mr. Founding Father, come to the stand! *(To the judge, as Founding Father comes forward.)* Your Honor, look at his hair—it's long and curly. He's wearing a wig! I want a pretty wig like that too! I want a long and curly wig!

JUDGE: Bailiff! Will you stop that nonsense and swear in the witness! *(To Founding Father.)* I must apologize for the bailiff's weird behavior, Mr. Founding Father . . .

BAILIFF: *(Handing the witness a copy of* Webster's New English Dictionary.*)* Place your left hand on this copy of *Webster's New English Dictionary* and close your right eye. Do you solemnly swear that the testimony you are about to give will be in English, wholly in English, and in nothing but English, so help you Webster?

WITNESS: Cross my heart and hope to die!

CHORUS: Cross my heart and hope to die!

BAILIFF: *(Curiously staring at the wig.)* Be seated!

JUDGE: *(Using the megaphone.)* The contestant for the prosecution can now begin questioning his celebrity witness.

PROSECUTOR: Thank you, Your Honor. As one of the Founding Fathers, do you believe that our government has the right—indeed, the responsibility—to defend our values, our ways and, especially, our language, from anyone threatening to change this great land of ours? And please, don't hesitate to dispense with the customary egalitarian rhetoric . . .

FOUNDING FATHER: We didn't make the American Revolution to let our nation become undermined by people of different languages, different ways, and different colors. It is an established historical fact that most of my fellow Founding Fathers felt torn between the American ideals of liberty and equality, on the one hand, and the more practical considerations of the time, on the other—if you know what I mean. Benjamin Franklin, of course, never having owned slaves, could well indulge in dreaming about extending full equality to all . . .

JUDGE: That answer is worth five points under the category of "Do as we preach, but not as we do" for the contestant for the prosecution, who again leads the game by the score of twenty-five to twenty!

LIBERTY: *(In a sensual, suggestive tone.)* And what about those rousing words of the Declaration of Independence: "We hold these truths to be self-evident, that all men are created equal, that they are endowed by their Creator with certain unalienable rights, that among these are Life, Liberty and the Pursuit of Happiness!" You know?

DEFENSE: Your Honor, with all due respect to the witness, his testimony must be placed within its proper perspective. We must remember that those were other times, that the Founding Fathers faced a different historical moment. Why, none other than our first president, George Washington himself, was a slaveholder. And so was Jefferson, the egalitarian author of the Declaration of Independence, whose views on Blacks and Indians certainly excluded them from consideration as equals. And who, Your Honor, would dare question these men's ideals? Who would dare question their patriotism?

LIBERTY: The defense's argument is unacceptable! What is morally abhorrent today, was also morally abhorrent in 1776. The weight of the historical evidence should clearly speak to America's collective conscience. The defense is making a mockery of America's judicial system! You know?

PROSECUTOR: *(To the witness.)* Then, based upon your recollections of the real intentions of the Founding Fathers, it is your expert opinion that they would have supported the English and English Only Act, right?

FOUNDING FATHER: Absolutely . . . you see, the Founding Fathers were realistic men of a practical nature—the Declaration of Independence notwithstanding. Besides, it is well recognized that all nations have the right to dictate the language which is to be spoken by their citizens within their borders. Let me put it this way: we have as much right to dictate that only English be spoken in America as, for example, Méjico has to require Spanish within its territory. Why, can you imagine anyone questioning the right of the Mexican government to dictate the use of Spanish in . . . let's say . . . Nuevo Méjico?

JUDGE: A point of clarification: Nuevo Méjico is no longer pronounced Nuevo Méjico—it is now pronounced New Mexico. *(Using the megaphone.)* New Mexico has been under the control of the United States since we took it from Mexico in 1848, and of course, Spanish has not been allowed to be spoken there since the passage of the English and English Only Act!

FOUNDING FATHER: No kidding . . . well, then what about Tejas? Doesn't the Mexican government have the sovereign right, if it so chooses, to dictate that Spanish be the only language of Tejas?

JUDGE: I beg your pardon, Mr. Founding Father, but Tejas is no longer pronounced Tejas—it is now pronounced Texas, and English is the official language there today. Oh, and of course, *(Using the megaphone.)* Texas has been part of these United States since 1845. Remember the Alamo?

CHORUS: Remember the Alamo!

FOUNDING FATHER: Well, can you then imagine anyone questioning the right of the Mexican government to require only Spanish in their territory of . . . California!

JUDGE: Mr. Founding Father, I am sorry, but I must inform you that California is no longer under the jurisdiction of the Mexican government. It has belonged to the United States since 1848; therefore, Spanish is no longer allowed there. *(Using the megaphone.)* English is now the only language allowed in California!

FOUNDING FATHER: Is that so . . . ? Well, can you then imagine anyone questioning the right of the Spanish government to insist that only Spanish be spoken in its territory of La Florida?

JUDGE: Again, I must correct you: La Florida is no longer pronounced La Florida—it is now pronounced Florida, and it ceased being a Spanish colony in 1819, when it became part of the United States. *(Using the megaphone.)* English is the only language spoken in . . .

FOUNDING FATHER: And how about the other territories that were first discovered by the Spaniards—what about Arizona, Nevada, Utah, Alabama, Colorado, Mississippi, and Oklahoma? Has the Spanish language also been banned from those territories?

JUDGE: I am afraid so! *(Using the megaphone.)* America is no longer composed of just thirteen small colonies. We have taken over all the territory from Canada in the north to the Rio Grande in the south. And of course, the United States also governs Alaska, Hawaii, the Virgin Islands, and Puerto Rico. Cha-cha-cha!

CHORUS: Cha-cha-cha!

FOUNDING FATHER: Alaska! The Russians do not own Alaska?

JUDGE: No, no, no, no, no, no . . .

CHORUS: No, no, no, no, no, no . . .

FOUNDING FATHER: Well, and what about Louisiana? Louisiana is still French, is it not?

JUDGE: I beg your pardon, but again, I must correct you: Louisiana is not French anymore. *(Using the megaphone.)* Louisiana is now part of the United States, and English is the only language spoken there today. And yes, let me add that Montana, Wyoming, the Dakotas, Nebraska, Iowa, Arkansas, Minnesota, Oklahoma, Missouri, and all the other North American territories that once belonged to France, also became part of the United States in 1803! Oh-la-la!

CHORUS: Oh-la-la!

FOUNDING FATHER: Are you telling me that the children of the children who once spoke Russian in Alaska, and French in Louisiana and all the Mississippi Valley, as well as those who once spoke Spanish in La Florida, Tejas, California, Arizona, Nevada, Colorado, Kansas, Utah, Nuevo Méjico, Puerto Rico, and parts of Alabama and Mississippi, are you telling me that now they are only allowed to speak English?

JUDGE: That's correct! *(Using the megaphone.)* The English and English Only Act is the supreme law of the land!

CHORUS: The English and English Only Act is the supreme law of the land!

FOUNDING FATHER: And the Indians? All those tribes which once roamed free, have they also been forced to give up their native languages?

JUDGE: *(Using the megaphone.)* Mr. Founding Father, I have just told you—repeatedly—that English and English only is allowed in the United States!

FOUNDING FATHER: Well, in that case, then . . . never mind . . .

JUDGE: I am sorry, but we must deduct five points from the score of the contestant for the prosecution, since his witness' testimony failed to support his case. So now the game is again tied at twenty points! Cha-cha-cha! *(Chorus repeats "cha-cha-cha.")* The contestant for the defense can now call his first celebrity witness.

LIBERTY: The forefathers of the defendant María Libertad not only brought the Spanish language when they settled in parts of La Florida, California, Tejas, Arizona, Alabama, Colorado, Kansas, Utah, Nuevo Méjico, and Puerto Rico, but by the time that the pilgrims landed at Plymouth Rock, the Spaniards had already established five universities, several printing presses, and hundreds of churches and schools in those territories which later became part of the United States. You know?

DEFENSE: Thank you, Your Honor. Since our argument in this trial is that the defendant, being so young and having such beautiful blonde hair and blue eyes, could easily pass for American after completing an Americanization Rehabilitation Program, I want to call Mr. Noble Savage as my first celebrity witness. It is the defense's contention that our policies toward the American Indian represent an example of the enlightened approach which we should also follow in the case of María Libertad.

JUDGE: Bailiff, please call Mr. Noble Savage . . .

BAILIFF: *(Blowing the whistle.)* Mr. Noble Savage, come to the stand!

CHORUS: *(Singing, as Noble Savage comes forward to the beat of Indian drums.)*

"Ten, little nine, little eight, little Indians;
seven, little six, little five, little Indians;

four, little three, little two, little Indians;
one little Indian boy."

BAILIFF: Your Honor, look! He's wearing a chicken on his head! Your Honor, Your Honor, I want a chicken too . . .

JUDGE: Bailiff, shut up and swear in the witness! *(To the audience.)* I must again apologize for the bailiff's . . . irregular behavior, but the new affirmative action quota system has forced us to hire the mentally deficient, like the bailiff, as well as the sexually versatile, *(Pointing to himself.)* like "you-know-who," as long as they can speak only English, of course . . .

BAILIFF: *(Handing the witness a book.)* Place your right hand on this copy of *Webster's New English Dictionary* and close your right eye. Mr. Noble Savage, do you solemnly swear that the testimony you are about to give will be in English, wholly in English, and in nothing but English, so help you Webster?

NOBLE SAVAGE: Cross my heart and hope to die!

CHORUS: Cross my heart and hope to die!

BAILIFF: Be seated!

JUDGE: *(Using the megaphone.)* The defense may now begin questioning his celebrity witness . . .

DEFENSE: Your Honor, we have always applied good old American ingenuity to resolve our problems within a spirit of fair play and compromise, as the testimony of Mr. Noble Savage will show. He will bear witness to the way in which we integrated the Indians into our nation. Your Honor, let's ask ourselves, what did our forefathers find in this great continent? Just a few Indian tribes in constant warfare with one another—and to them, we gave our language, our customs, and our religion. We tried to make Americans out of them, did we not?

PROSECUTOR: I object, Your Honor; I fail to see the relevance of the defense's line of argument. Besides, will you remind the defense that the Indians, after all, were already here, and we were more or less stuck with them? But María Libertad is a foreigner!

DEFENSE: What! María Libertad a foreigner! Is the prosecution questioning the investigation conducted by the English and English Only Enforcement Agency? Is the prosecution going to ignore that said investigation revealed that María Libertad was born in a cave deep within the Rocky Mountains? Your Honor, the last time I checked my geography, that land had been part of the United

States since 1848, when it was taken from Mexico. Will you explain to the prosecution that that makes the defendant also an American by birthright—although not culturally speaking, I must concede.

JUDGE: I am going to have to overrule the objection of the contestant for the prosecution and take away five points from his score. So now for the first time the contestant for the defense has taken the lead.

DEFENSE: Your Honor, allow me to call the Court's attention to the policies towards the Indians which guided our government. *(To Noble Savage, patronizing.)* I am referring to the way in which the Great White father in Washington tried to Americanize your people. Yes, Mr. Noble Savage, I want you to tell this court how our government shipped off your children to boarding schools and kept them away from their families to help speed up their Americanization. Your Honor, we can do the same thing with María Libertad!

NOBLE SAVAGE: Anything Indian was taken away from them. When they returned, they spoke only English, wore store-bought clothes, and cut their hair short, but to the white people they were still Indians—and to their families in the reservations, they had become strangers. *(To the audience.)* Instead of war paint, our young braves began making up their faces with Cover Girl and Revlon, and our maidens crossed their hearts with Maidenform . . .

PROSECUTOR: Your Honor, if we are going to start paying attention to this Indian, next we will be wrestling alligators and wearing nothing but a loincloth! This court must uphold the law . . . We cannot allow this girl just to get by with some new fashions, a different haircut, and a brassiere that lifts and separates!

BAILIFF: *(Blows the whistle.)* Scalp her! Scalp her! Your Honor, I want a blonde wig made out of her beautiful long hair . . .

CHORUS: Scalp her! Scalp her!

JUDGE: Bailiff! *(To the defense.)* I must confess that the Indian's testimony is also making me feel some reservation—no pun intended. *(To the audience.)* "Indian" . . . "reservation," don't you get it?

LIBERTY: The Indians could probably have survived losing their lands and everything else, but not the pride in their cultural identity.

Once their culture was taken away, they began to disappear from the face of America . . . You know?

NOBLE SAVAGE: Brother, the Great Spirit made us all, but he made a great difference between his white and red children. He gave us a different complexion and different customs. Since he made so great a difference between us in other things, why may we not conclude that he gave us a different language according to the designs of Mother Nature? The Great Spirit has always done right; he knows what is best for his children.

PROSECUTOR: The Great Spirit! The Great Spirit! Your Honor, this Indian is invoking the Great Spirit! Are we going to have to listen to this kind of irreverent voodoo mumbo jumbo? In God's name, Your Honor, would you tell the witness to get to the point! *(To Noble Savage.)* Redskin, you speak with a forked tongue!

BAILIFF: *(Blowing his whistle.)* Cut his tongue off! Cut his tongue off!

CHORUS: Cut his tongue off! Cut his tongue off!

JUDGE: Silence! *(To Noble Savage.)* Witness, you must stop talking about the Great Spirit! *(Using the megaphone.)* Don't you understand this is a Christian trial?

NOBLE SAVAGE: Brother, we do not understand these things. We were told that your language was given to your forefathers and had been handed down from father to son. Once, we also had a language which was given to our forefathers and had been handed down from father to son. We did not wish to destroy your language; we only wanted to enjoy our own. Listen, Brother, all we wanted was to be left alone to enjoy Mother Nature. *(Pause.)* It's not nice to fool Mother Nature . . .

PROSECUTOR: I object, Your Honor, on the grounds that, contrary to the defense's contention, the Indians have not really disappeared into America's melting pot—just look at the cowboy pictures!

JUDGE: Objection sustained! This witness is dismissed and the contestant for the defense loses five points! And again, our game is tied at fifteen points!

BAILIFF: Your Honor, when you mentioned melting pot I got awfully hungry . . . When do we eat?

CHORUS: When do we eat? When do we eat? When do we eat? When do we eat? When do we eat?

JUDGE: *(Over the Chorus.)* Order! Order in the Court! *(To the audience, using the megaphone.)* While we restore order in here, we will take a brief commercial break. Don't you go away, 'cause we'll be right back and continue playing "The Great American Justice Game"!

Black out and cut to pre-taped TV commercial.

COMMERCIAL

ANNOUNCER: Remember those old movie classics that you enjoyed as a child? Movies like *Gone with the Wind*, *Fiddler on the Roof*, *Westside Story*, and other all-time favorites?

Well, now you can increase your viewing pleasure! That's right, you can now watch your favorite movies again and again without having to sit through those bothersome scenes showing Blacks, Jews, Puerto Ricans, and other minorities who are not one hundred percent Americans. . . .

How is that possible? Well, using a new computer, WASPish Movie Classics has been able to decolorize Blacks, make Jewish noses straight, and take that ugly accent out of Spanish garble.

So, bring your family together, take a six-pack out of the refrigerator, and get ready to really enjoy *Gone with the Wind* with an all-white cast, *Fiddler on the Roof* without crooked noses, or *Westside Story* in perfect English . . . How sweet it is!

VOICE OVER: WASPish Movie Classics, now available exclusively through the network of KKK retail stores right in your own neighborhood.

SCENE 3

JUDGE: Welcome back again to "The Great American Justice Game"! With the score even at fifteen points, it is now time for the contest . . . *(The Judge is interrupted by the singing of a religious hymn.)* Bailiff! What's that noise?

BAILIFF: It's someone singing . . . dua-dua-duaa . . .

CHORUS: Dua-dua-duaa . . .

JUDGE: I know it's someone singing "dua-dua-duaa," but . . .

UNCLE TOM: *(Enters singing with religious fervor.)*

"When I can read my title clear
To mansions in the skies,

I'll bid farewell to every fear,
And wipe my weeping eyes."

BAILIFF: Who the hell is this?

JUDGE: Bailiff! Control yourself! *(Using the megaphone.)* It's nobody—just a Negro . . .

CHORUS: It's nobody—just a Negro . . .

UNCLE TOM: *(Jiving.)* I's poor ol' Uncle Tom, Mas'er. I belong to Mas'er George—a more fine gentleman you could never meet. Oh, and I be coming from my cabin, you know, the one that my good mas'er gave me. *(Begins singing again.)*

"My soul is soaring high,
To the big cabin in the sky.
In the sky, in the sky . . . "

JUDGE: Silence! Who let this . . . this . . . this . . . well, this . . . Negro in here? Get him out of here before he starts singing again! *(Mocking.)* Dua-duaa!

CHORUS: Dua-duaa!

DEFENSE: Your Honor, with the permission of the Court, I would like to ask Mr. Uncle Tom a few questions . . .

JUDGE: If the contestant for the prosecution has no objections, I will let you question the Negro. Bailiff, please swear in the witness . . .

BAILIFF: *(Blowing his whistle and handing him a book.)* Place your left hand on this copy of *Webster's New English Dictionary* and close your right eye. Do you solemnly swear that the testimony you are about to give will be in English, wholly in English, and in nothing but English, so help you Webster?

UNCLE TOM: I's sorry, Mas'er, but this book here is no Bible . . .

DEFENSE: Your Honor, allow me . . . Mr. Uncle Tom, I appreciate your religious feelings, but a young girl is on trial and your testimony may help decide her fate. Please, just say "cross my heart and hope to die," just as if you were singing . . .

UNCLE TOM: Mas'er knows that song too? *(Uncle Tom begins singing with fervor.)*

"If I can hear His calling clear,
In fields of lilies I shall lie,
For life no longer I do fear,
Cross my heart and hope to die."

CHORUS: Cross my heart and hope to die!

DEFENSE: There you are, Your Honor: he said it. I clearly heard him say "cross my heart and hope to die."

JUDGE: You can then proceed to question the witness.

DEFENSE: Mr. Uncle Tom, where were you born?

UNCLE TOM: Don't know for certain . . . but I reckon it was in Africa . . .

DEFENSE: Well, if you were not born in the United States, then your native language was not English. Is that correct?

UNCLE TOM: You's right, Mas'er.

JUDGE: I don't see where this testimony is taking us.

DEFENSE: Your Honor, my point is that if Mr. Uncle Tom, who was born in some uncivilized corner of the Dark Continent, and probably never spoke a real language before learning English, if this unfortunate creature found a place in American society, is it too much to ask that we give María Libertad at least the same opportunity to learn English and find a place among us? After all, Your Honor, with the severe shortage of dishwashers, maids, and—shall we say—ladies of the evening, doesn't it stand to reason that the defendant has a contribution to make . . .

UNCLE TOM: I don't understand why they be fussing. I was a slave all my life, and I sure's glad how my mas'er treated me. He learned me English, and he learned me to read this here Bible . . . he gave me religion . . .

DEFENSE: Did you hear that, Your Honor? The witness fully recognizes that it is possible to learn English. And if an imported Negro like Uncle Tom can learn to speak and read English, surely this girl can too! After all, the girl is white . . .

JUDGE: And that argument is worth five points to the contestant for the defense under the category of "Whatever a coon can do, a honky can do better"! The contestant for the defense is leading again by the score of twenty to fifteen! This witness is excused! Dua-duaa!

CHORUS: Dua-duaa!

UNCLE TOM: *(As he walks away, singing.)*

We shall overcome,
the day we die,
'cause up in heaven,
we'll all be white.

We shall overcome,
the day we die,
for our Lord Jesus,
is color blind.

LIBERTY: What happened to those immortal words: "A man should not be judged by the color of his skin, but by the content of his character? You know? Why did we let the dream die? Must we continue to put up with this charade?

CHORUS: Charade!

PROSECUTOR AND DEFENSE: Charade!

JUDGE: Charade! Remember, the contestant with the correct answer to this "charade" will score five points and will also call the next witness . . . And the hint for today's correct answer is a true statement which is frequently repeated among full-blooded Americans . . . a six- to eight-word sentence . . . *(Using the megaphone.)* Ready? Set! Go!

PROSECUTOR: "At night, all cats are black!"

CHORUS: *(Like an echo.)* At night, all cats are black!

JUDGE: True, but it's the wrong answer! Dua-duaa! Next!

CHORUS: Dua-duaa!

DEFENSE: "The Anglos get richer and the poor have children!"

CHORUS: The Anglos get richer and the poor have children!

JUDGE: Close, but not the correct answer!

PROSECUTOR: "Bilingualism is an incurable disease!"

CHORUS: Bilingualism is an incurable disease!

JUDGE: That was very close! The contestant for the prosecution keeps getting closer and closer . . . Cha-cha-cha!

CHORUS: Cha-cha-cha!

PROSECUTOR: "The greasier their hair, the funnier their accent!"

CHORUS: The greasier their hair, the funnier their accent!

JUDGE: Right! That correct answer is worth five full points for the contestant for the prosecution under the category of "This is a Charade"! And having again tied the game, he will get an opportunity to call the next celebrity witness!

LIBERTY: It is inconceivable that we forget that in rejecting the black, the brown, the yellow, the red, and all but the white, we repudiate America's origins and ideals . . . You know?

PROSECUTOR: Thank you, Your Honor. I am proud to call on Mr. White Supremacist as my next and last celebrity witness!

BAILIFF: *(Blowing his whistle.)* Will Mr. White Supremacist come to the stand! *(White Supremacist, wearing white hood and robe, comes forth.)* Your Honor, he's wearing a hood to cover his hair! I want a hood like that too!

JUDGE: What are you waiting for? Swear him in!

BAILIFF: *(Handing the witness a book.)* Place your left hand on this copy of *Webster's New English Dictionary* and close your right eye. Do you solemnly swear that the testimony you are about to give will be in English, wholly in English, and in nothing but English, so help you Webster?

SUPREMACIST: Cross my heart and hope to die! Proudly so . . .

CHORUS: Cross my heart and hope to die!

BAILIFF: Be seated!

JUDGE: *(To the prosecutor.)* Your witness . . .

PROSECUTOR: I purposely left Mr. White Supremacist for last, because I want to leave fresh in the memory of this court the patriotic testimony which is embodied in the principles of one hundred percent Americanism . . .

SUPREMACIST: And proud of it! The Ku Klux Klan has proudly embodied the principles of one hundred percent Americanism, proudly upheld the tenets of the Christian religion, proudly defended the virtues of pure manhood, and equally proudly supported the ideals of racial purity! Had America heeded our message, this nation would never have fallen into the so-called "era of the civil rights movement." Indeed our darkest hour was when our mothers, sisters, and daughters had to suffer the glorification of that which was not only alien, but actually un-American and actively anti-American!

JUDGE: Well said! That answer is worth five points to the contestant for the prosecution under the category of "Whiteness is next to godliness." And with the score at twenty-five to twenty, the contestant for the prosecution takes the lead one more time! Proceed please . . .

LIBERTY: "One hundred percent Americanism" should not be allowed to become a code word for rationalizing the denial of equal educational opportunities to minority children or their cultural castration, or for justifying mob lynchings of innocent Blacks, or for encouraging the bombing of churches! You know?

PROSECUTOR: Thank you, Your Honor. *(To White Supremacist.)* The principles of one hundred percent Americanism . . . Mr. White Supremacist, does the English and English Only Act of 1990 promote the principles of one hundred percent Americanism?

SUPREMACIST: Is the kettle black? *(The Chorus repeats "Is the kettle black?")* Of course! Every instinct, every dictate of conscience and public spirit, insists that we proudly defend the principles of one hundred percent Americanism against the Negro, ever anxious to prey upon the purity of white women; against the parasitic Jewish shopkeeper; against the Papist priest, loyal not to America but to Rome; and of course, against the most dangerous of all invaders, the alien, for overtly attempting to change America by means of the silly but deadly philosophy of cultural pluralism.

JUDGE: Five more points to the score of the contestant of the prosecution under the category of "Never let the facts confuse the issue." He has now extended his lead to ten points. Before excusing the witness, I want to direct a last question to him: Do you believe that the defendant, María Libertad, poses a threat to the principles of one hundred percent Americanism?

SUPREMACIST: Are the spics greasy? *(The Chorus repeats "Are the spics greasy?")* Of course! Had such people not been stopped, then white, English-speaking, Anglo-Saxon Protestants would have become a minority in the land of their forefathers, and today, America would have become culturally transformed.

LIBERTY: And what about the Constitution? Have we forgotten that the Bill of Rights was a historical answer to the fact that America has always been a nation of immigrants? You know?

BAILIFF: Your Honor, Your Honor, I also have a question, may I . . . pretty please? Can he take off his hood? I want to see his hair . . .

SUPREMACIST: Proudly! This hood and this robe are the regalia of the order and the shield that protects the crusade of the Invisible Empire! *(White Supremacist takes off the hood to reveal the face of Hitler.)*

BAILIFF: *(Blowing the whistle.)* Heil Hitler! Heil Hitler! Your Honor, Your Honor, it is the Führer!

CHORUS: Heil Hitler! Heil Hitler! It's the Führer!

PROSECUTOR: *(Getting carried away.)* Heil Hitler!

JUDGE: *(To the prosecution.)* What are you doing?

PROSECUTOR: I cannot help being what I am. I am neither a Jew, nor a

Negro, nor a foreigner, I am an English-speaking, Anglo-Saxon white man, so ordained by the hand and will of God, and I can't help that, as a pure American, I will not accept any customs, any religions, or any languages brought by some inferior ass from a remote corner on the other side of the world!

DEFENSE: Your Honor, all of this is getting to be a bit too much . . . It is my humble opinion that this time . . .

JUDGE: I am sorry, but "this time" the contestant for the defense is out of time, 'cause we must cut to a commercial. So, with the contestant for the prosecution ahead by a score of thirty to twenty, we will be right back for the exciting final segment of "The Great American Justice Game!"

Black out and cut to pre-taped TV commercial.

COMMERCIAL

ANNOUNCER: Tired of those menial, dirty domestic chores that used to be done by immigrants, refugees, wetbacks, and illegal aliens? Chores such as scrubbing your toilets, mowing the lawn, picking up the mess your kids leave behind, and yes, even cleaning windows!

Well, now there is an easier way to get it done. That's right, Sears has introduced a new line of domestic robots designed to replace most common varieties of foreign servants. Just think of it! Order the model of your choice from the Sears Catalog, put it to work, and you'll never again be embarrassed by the ugly sight of your servants' dirty hands and sweaty armpits.

The economy model, the "Señorita," is the perfect robot for all cleaning jobs in the home. Just turn the control switch to the task you need, and then sit and relax while your own "Señorita" leaves your home sparkling clean. But there's more: the Señorita does it without uttering a single Spanish word.

And for the gentleman of the house, we have the "Susie Wong" model. It comes only in yellow, and is ideal for doing the laundry, massaging your back, and performing exotic sensual dances.

There is also the top of the line "Filipino Couple," sold only in sets of two, which can perform the jobs of butler and housekeeper. This set is finished in the likeness of Ferdinand and Imelda Marcos to add a touch of class to your home.

VOICE OVER: Rechargeable batteries for all robots and shoes for the Imelda Marcos model can be ordered separately from Sears.

Sears, where white America shops!

SCENE 4

JUDGE: Welcome back again to "The Great American Justice Game"! As we begin the final segment of our show, the contestant for the prosecution is ahead by the score of thirty to twenty. Obviously, the fate of today's defendant, María Libertad, is beginning to look very bad. But now, the contestant for the defense will get a chance to call his last celebrity witness. *(Using the megaphone.)* Is the contestant for the defense ready?

DEFENSE: Yes, Your Honor. As my last celebrity witness I want to call a man who is faster than a speeding bullet . . .

BAILIFF: Faster than a nigger running from a lynch mob?

CHORUS: Faster than a nigger running from a lynch mob . . .

JUDGE: Bailiff!

DEFENSE: A man more powerful than a locomotive . . .

BAILIFF: More powerful than the sexual drive of a Puerto Rican on Spanish fly?

CHORUS: More powerful than the sexual drive of a Puerto Rican on Spanish fly . . .

JUDGE: Bailiff! Don't you know when to shut up? *(Motioning to the defense to continue.)*

DEFENSE: A man capable of leaping over tall buildings in a single bound . . .

BAILIFF: Like a Mexican jumping over the Rio Grande to cross the border!

CHORUS: Like a Mexican jumping over the Rio Grande to cross the border . . .

JUDGE: Bailiff, one more interruption from you and I'll have you transferred to family court in Spanish Harlem! *(To the defense.)* Will the contestant for the defense please identify his witness? Cha-cha-chaa!

CHORUS: Cha-cha-chaa!

DEFENSE: Your Honor, I am, of course, referring to Superman!

JUDGE: *(Using the megaphone.)* Bailiff, please call Superman to the stand.

BAILIFF: *(Blowing his whistle.)* Superman, come to the stand! *(Handing Superman a book.)* Place your left hand on this copy of *Webster's New English Dictionary* and close your right eye. Do you solemnly swear that the testimony you are about to give will be in English, wholly in English, and in nothing but English, so help you Webster?

SUPERMAN: Cross my heart and hope to die!

CHORUS: Cross my heart and hope to die!

JUDGE: The contestant for the defense may now proceed to question his witness . . .

DEFENSE: Thank you, Your Honor. Superman, I have only one question for you: how many languages do you speak?

SUPERMAN: Well, it's hard to tell, but my adventures are told in more than a dozen languages to people from approximately one hundred countries—that's what makes me the most universal of all American heroes. Of course, having been born on the planet Krypton, my native language is really Kryptonian.

DEFENSE: There you are, Your Honor! The man who stands as a universal symbol of freedom, justice, and the American way of life, has just testified that he speaks more than a dozen languages and that his native tongue is not even English, but Kryptonian!

PROSECUTOR: I object, Your Honor! I object! The testimony of this witness should be stricken from the record on the grounds that Superman is really an illegal alien!

CHORUS: Superman is really an illegal alien!

JUDGE: Objection sustained! The witness is excused!

BAILIFF: But I like Superman . . .

JUDGE: Well, this game . . . I mean . . . trial is quickly approaching its conclusion, and since there are no more witnesses, it's time now for both contestants to present their final arguments, which can be worth up to twenty full points. First, the contestant for the prosecution will get his chance to deliver the closing statement.

PROSECUTOR: My fellow Americans, we are God's chosen people! In 1789, America was limited to just thirteen states, but we responded to the Anglo-Saxon calling within us and the march of the American way of life swept from ocean to ocean until God's chosen people could, in time, celebrate that the Indians became civilized and the Blacks were emancipated and the Hispanics were taught English—and they all were given the opportunity to participate in the American way of life.

CHORUS: *(Singing.)* And the march of the American way went on and on!

LIBERTY: *(Over the humming of the Chorus.)* My God, how can we forget the contributions which each of those groups has made to the development of America? There need not be a conflict between being Indian or Black or Hispanic, and also being American! You know?

CHORUS: *(Marching and singing.)* And the march of the American way went on and on!

PROSECUTOR: *(Over the humming of the Chorus.)* And then, despite the constant triumphal march of the American way of life, our destiny was challenged, not by the enemies beyond our borders, but challenged from within, challenged by those ingrates whose misery we replaced with America's plenty, and whose chaos and tyranny were swept away by the highest honor liberty can bestow: citizenship in the great American Republic!

CHORUS: *(Again marching and singing.)* And the march of the American way went on and on!

PROSECUTOR: *(Over the humming of the Chorus.)* Those ingrates—immigrants, illegal aliens, refugees, and wetbacks—made attempts against the American way of life as God has revealed it, threatening our traditions, our language, and our culture.

CHORUS: *(Marching and singing.)* And the march of the American way went on and on!

PROSECUTOR: *(Over the humming of the Chorus.)* The girl on trial today for violating the English and English Only Act represents the reincarnation of that threat. She is the enemy, and her language and culture are her deadly weapons. Make no mistake about it. Anything but the full sentence prescribed by the law would signal that our faith in the American way has weakened. It would be an invitation for the resurgence of cultural pluralism and bilingualism, not to mention the return of the Mexican taco, the Cuban sandwich, and Puerto Rican rum!

CHORUS: *(Marching and singing in crescendo.)* And the march of the American way went on and on!

PROSECUTOR: *(Over the humming of the Chorus.)* My fellow Americans, as God's chosen people we cannot shrink from our sacred duties, for it is ours to execute the fate that has driven us to be greater than any other nation. We cannot allow any retreat from the path that leads to the fulfillment of God's manifest destiny, and that destiny is written in the English language and only in the English language!

CHORUS: *(Concluding the marching song.)* And the march of the American way went on and on! And the march of the American way went on and on!

JUDGE: Hallelujah! That closing statement is worth the full twenty points for the contestant for the prosecution, who continues increasing his lead.

LIBERTY: *(In a lusty and seductive tone.)* How in God's name can we justify putting limits on man's expression as a leash is put on a dog or a chastity belt on a whore, and then pretend that we have changed their nature? To restrict the freedom of expression of just one girl is to question the spontaneous manifestation of life itself. To impose a common denominator, be it a uniform language or a homogenized culture, is to brutalize our senses and to cry out against the very miracle of creation. You know? Ladies and gentlemen, let's stand up and cheer: "Vive la différence!"

CHORUS: Vive la différence!

JUDGE: And now we will hear the closing statement from the contestant for the defense.

DEFENSE: The English and English Only Act of 1990, Your Honor, does not appear to take into account that in English the word "language" has two different meanings, which are so distinct as to provoke semantic ambiguity. In one interpretation, the word has a plural (namely, languages) and may be preceded by the definite or indefinite article. The other interpretation has no plural, and is never preceded by any article.

PROSECUTOR: I object, Your Honor! The defense's argument is not only irrelevant, but also difficult to follow . . .

JUDGE: Objection sustained! The contestant for the defense loses five points and is risking disqualification if his closing statement does not address the issues of this trial in a more relevant manner!

LIBERTY: The fundamental issue here is freedom of expression, which is the cornerstone of America! I never thought that this would come to pass! You know? *(Crying.)* God, why has the American dream become a nightmare?

CHORUS: Why has the American dream become a nightmare?

DEFENSE: Your Honor, such morphological and syntactic distinctions are indeed relevant since they have semantic implications. When referring to "a language," one means a conventional system of speech practiced throughout a rather extensive community, such as English or Latin. Those are "languages" in the popular meaning of the term. To refer to "language," however, is to speak of something much broader. In what sense "much broader"? Well, in the same sense as "I like dancing" is to make a much broader statement than "I like this type of dance," when speaking, for example, of the waltz. Dancing, broadly speaking, may indeed be to my liking—although I may dislike a particular dance . . .

LIBERTY: My God! I can't believe that this is happening in America! What kind of defense argument is that? A girl's life is being decided, and the defense, all of a sudden, gets the urge to go dancing! You know? This whole trial has been a Mickey Mouse affair!

CHORUS: A Mickey Mouse affair! *(Singing the Mickey Mouse Mouseketeers' song.)* M—I—C—K—E—Y, M—O—U—S—E . . . Mickey Mouse, Mickey Mouse . . . *(The Chorus gets excited and sings the Mouseketeers' song louder and louder.)*

JUDGE: Order! Order! *(Raps the gavel three times.)*

Quick blackout: at this point there is complete silence for an instant, then the rapping of the gavel is heard again as if someone were knocking on a door. A spotlight begins shining on María Libertad, who seems to be sleeping.

LIBERTY: Mickey . . . Mickey Mouse . . . ! *(Off stage, as if she were calling María Libertad.)*

MARIA: *(Waking up, alarmed and confused.)* Mickey Mouse! Mickey Mouse!

LIBERTY: *(Enters.)* But María, you've fallen asleep and haven't put on the Mickey Mouse costume yet! Come on, hurry up! We're going to be late for the Halloween party . . . You know?

MARIA: Mamá, Mamá! I had an awful dream! A nightmare!

LIBERTY: Come on, hurry up! Your father's already dressed up and waiting! You know? You should see him—he looks so proud wearing his Ponce de León costume! *(To the public.)* Wow . . . I bet that tonight he is going to sing me those old Spanish songs that drive me . . .

MARIA: *(Hysterical, interrupting her mother.)* Mamá! Mamá! I dreamed that we could no longer speak Spanish—that it was illegal—and that I was involved in this horrible trial because . . . It was awful, Mamá, it was so awful . . .

LIBERTY: María, cálmate . . . You were just dreaming, baby . . . You don't have to be afraid . . . This is America, you know, the land of the free!

Chorus begins humming "America the Beautiful."

MARIA: But Mamá, it all seemed so real!

LIBERTY: Mi amor, estamos en América! That could never happen here . . . You know? It was just a bad nightmare . . . Ven, déjame darte un beso. *(They embrace.)*

MARIA: *(Beginning to relax.)* And you were also in my nightmare, Mamá—wearing your Statue of Liberty costume . . . You were the sexiest Statue of Liberty that I ever saw!

LIBERTY: *(To the public, in a sexy tone.)* Then for sure my Ponce de León will sing me the old Spanish songs tonight. Bilinguals can do it in two tongues, you know?

MARIA: Mamá, qué bueno que somos americanos! I am so proud to be an American! *(Stage lights come on again as María puts on the Mouseketeers' ears and runs to take the megaphone away from the Judge; then she yells to the audience.)* I'm so proud to be an American! Give me an "A!"

CHORUS: "A!"

MARIA: Give me an "M!"

CHORUS: "M!"

MARIA: Give me an "E!"

CHORUS: "E!"

MARIA: Give me an "R!"

CHORUS: "R!"

MARIA: Give me an "I!"

CHORUS: "I!"

MARIA: Give me a "C!"

CHORUS: "C!"

MARIA: Give me an "A!"

CHORUS: "A!"

MARIA: Give me a "U!"

CHORUS: "U!"
MARIA: Give me an "S!"
CHORUS: "S!"
MARIA: Give me an "A!"
CHORUS: "A!"
MARIA: And, what do you get?
CHORUS: *Singing to the Mouseketeers' tune, the entire cast joins in singing and parading with great joy. Fireworks go off, and red, white, and blue balloons are released into the audience.)*

A—M—E—R—I—C—A for U—S—A!
U—S—A! U—S—A!
Where freedom and justice does prevail!
A—M—E—R—I—C—A for U—S—A!
U—S—A . . . U—S—A
The land of hope and faith!
A—M—E—R—I—C—A for U—S—A!
U—S—A! U—S—A!

Blackout. Curtain falls.

Traitor

Reinaldo Arenas

Reinaldo Arenas

Born in Holguín, province of Oriente, in 1943, Reinaldo Arenas published his first novel, *Celestino antes del alba,* in 1967. Other novels followed: *El mundo alucinante* (1969), *El palacio de las blanquísimas mofetas* (1980), *Otra vez el mar* (1982), *Arturo, la estrella más brillante* (1984), *La loma del Angel* (1987), *Viaje a La Habana* (1990), *El portero* (1990), *El color del verano* (1991), and *El asalto* (1991). A very versatile author, Arenas also published short stories, *Termina el desfile* (1982); poetry, *El central* (1981); and theater, *Persecución* (1986). In 1969 he was selected by the French literary critics as the best foreign novelist published in France. To date his works have been translated into ten different languages. Reinaldo Arenas committed suicide on December 7, 1990, in anticipation of the inevitable outcome of the Acquired Immune Deficiency Syndrome from which he had been suffering for several years.

Arenas always used Spanish as his literary language. His hardships as a writer in Castro's Cuba, as well as various differences of an intellectual and personal nature with the regime, including his imprisonment there, left their imprint on the works written after his departure in 1980 during the notorious Mariel exodus. Arenas was perhaps the most militant Cuban writer in exile. He missed no opportunity to speak out for Cuba's intellectual and political freedom.

Traitor is one of five short plays included in his book, *Persecución* (Miami: Ediciones Universal, 1986). Really a monologue delivered by the "Old Woman," it recounts the true story of the "traitor." The action takes place in Cuba at that imaginary moment when Castro's regime has come to an end. Through the eyes of the Old Woman, the play presents a grim picture of everyday life in Communist Cuba. Not only does she evoke that life, but she also gives us the perspective of the man whose tale she tells. Paradoxically, by his internal rebellion against everything that surrounds him, he has become an exemplary participant in the revolutionary process. *Traitor* is the tragic story of a man whose life has been ruled by hatred and fear, but whose apparent obedience—actually born of resentment—to the overthrown regime brings about his own fall.

Traitor

Characters

A seventy-year-old woman.
A journalist, an impersonal young man.
A technician or assistant, middle aged, absolutely impersonal, absorbed in his work.

Stage Effects

At the rear of the stage there will be a motion picture screen on which different images will be projected at the indicated time. For the role of the woman, though it is not mandatory, a man made up like an old woman is recommended. The journalist will wear office clothes (long-sleeved shirt, tie); the technician will wear an overall or some other work clothes. The characters cannot appear grotesque.

Setting

The action takes place in a room of an Old Havana house. There is an old rocking chair with a small table in front of it, and a chair on the other side. Stage left, a flower pot with a small withered palm. Stage rear, the screen which also functions as a large white wall. Crossing the entire stage front, an enormous rope, taut and tied at both ends. It will give the scene a feeling of confinement.

As the curtain rises, Chopin's Study No. 1, Opus 10, somewhat frantic, will be heard while the stage is prepared in full view of the audience. The old woman will already be seated. The journalist and technician will move around her in a professional manner with different pieces of equipment: cameras, lights, cables, microphones, recorders, white laminated boards that will be used in the lighting, etc. They are preparing to film an interview. The journalist has just placed another small recorder on the table next to where the woman is seated. She observes all the bustle about her, but without much interest. The impression should be created that the old woman is being besieged by the strange and decidedly aggressive devices. The journalist and technician will exchange opinions that the audience cannot hear. For a moment, all the lights go out. The music ends. There is absolute darkness and silence. Gradually the lights that surround the old woman come on. These lights and those on the screen (when it is used) will constitute the lighting for this work. The director may use these lights in accord with the changes in the monologue—sometimes brighter, other times, fainter. The screen in back of the characters will function as a visual flashback as well as a simple screen which will sometimes reflect what the old woman has just said. During the interview, the journalist can stand, take a photograph, take notes. The technician will watch over the working of the equipment.

All of the equipment is now in place. The journalist sits down, facing the old woman. The technician works the camera. The woman begins to speak.

OLD WOMAN: I'll speak quickly and poorly so don't think you'll accomplish much with your little machine. Don't think you're going to get much out of what I might say and that later you'll fix it here and there, adding this or that, and come up with a book, or whatever, and become famous at my expense . . . Although, I don't know. Maybe if I speak badly, the thing might be even better for you. People could like it even more. You could exploit it more . . . because I can see you're the devil . . . But since you're here with those gadgets, I'll talk. A little, almost nothing. Only to show you that without us, you're nothing. The ash tray's there, under the chair. Get it if you want . . . Such a lot of equipment, a really clean shirt . . . *(She feels the shirt with her fingers.)* Is it silk? . . . Is silk back? . . . But well . . . I guess your duty is to stay there standing, or seated on that chair with a broken seat—yes, I know they're selling replacement seats—and ask me questions.

SCREEN: Stupendous parade, gigantic concentration of people, thousands of flags. View of Revolution Square, crowded with people. At the rear, the grandstand with high ranking military officers.

Fidel Castro in the paroxysm of a speech. Ovation. *(The screen becomes dark.)*

OLD WOMAN: *(Taking up her monologue again.)* What do you know? What does anyone know? Now that the dictator has fallen, was overthrown, or got tired, everyone talks, everyone can talk. The system has changed again. Ah, now everybody's a hero. Now it turns out that everyone was against him. But in those days when there was a surveillance committee on every corner that night and day watched the doors of every house, the windows, the walls, the lights, the darkness, and all our movements, and all our words, and all our silences, and what we heard on the radio, and what we didn't hear, and who our friends were, and who, our enemies, and what our sex life was like, and our correspondence, and our illnesses, and our dreams . . . All of that was checked too. Ah, but I see that you don't believe me. I'm old. Think that way if you like. I'm old and I talk nonsense. Think that way. It's better. Now a person can think, don't you understand me? Don't you realize that in those days you couldn't even think? But now you can, can't you? Of course, you can. And that would be a matter of concern, if anything could concern me at this point. If you're allowed to speak your mind today, it's because there's nothing to criticize, nothing to say. Otherwise, they . . . *(She points instinctively to the screen.)* they'd stop you. Well, listen to me, *they* are here. *(She points to the rear of the stage.) They* have poisoned everything, and they're everywhere . . . Now, whatever'll be done will be because of *them.* For or against them, but always because of them.

SCREEN: Hymns. Grandiose military parade. Squadrons pass by, marching in a martial fashion, lifting their feet at a ninety-degree angle, all this before the grandstand. Cries are heard of "Commander in Chief, order! Hurrah! Hurrah! Hurrah!" *(The screen becomes dark.)*

OLD WOMAN: What do I say? What am I saying? Is it true that I can say whatever I want? Is it really true? Tell me. At first it hardly seemed possible to me. I still don't believe it. Times change. Once again I hear people talk of liberty. They even shout it. That's bad. When one shouts "liberty" that way, generally the opposite's desired. I know. I saw . . . You came and found me. You're here with those gadgets for some reason. Do they work? Really?

Look, I'm not going to repeat myself. There are more than enough people around to make things up . . . Now come the declarations. Of course, everybody talks. Everybody makes a fuss. Everybody squeals. Everybody was—how nice!—against the tyranny. And I don't doubt it. Ah, but in those times, who didn't wear a distinctive political button awarded, naturally, by the regime? Check it out carefully. By the way, wasn't your father a militiaman?[1] Didn't he do . . . the voluntary work? *Voluntary.* That was the word. With Castro's overthrow, I myself was on the point of being shot as a Castroite. How horrible! Letters I'd sent to my sister in exile saved me. And if those letters hadn't existed? . . . She had to send them to me quickly, otherwise they'd have killed me. I haven't gone out since, because some, no, *a lot* of that has remained in the air. And I don't want to smell it. I . . .

SCREEN: A man appears handcuffed. Behind him stands a group of soldiers with rifles. Whistles and shouts of "Paredón, paredón, paredón!"[2] *(The screen becomes dark.)*

OLD WOMAN: You're asking me to speak, to contribute, to cooperate by saying what I know, since you intend to write a book, or something similar, about one of the victims . . . or should one say, a "double victim" . . . or "triple" . . . or rather a "victimized victim"? Anyhow, you decide. You can write whatever you please. It's not necessary for me to look it over. I don't want to change anything. At any rate, I'm taking advantage of this freedom of "expression"—is it still said that way?—to tell you that you're a buzzard. Have they gotten rid of all of them too? Aren't they necessary anymore? What birds! They fed off the rotting flesh of the corpses, and then, they'd fly up in the sky as if they were carrying the souls in their beaks. . . . And why did they exterminate them? They kept the island clean under all the regimes. How they gulped things down! Maybe they died poisoned from eating the corpses of the criminals sentenced by you to die—*sentenced,* is that still the word? . . . But listen, bring that machine closer, quickly. I'm in a hurry, old and tired and, to be frank, I'm also poisoned . . . Before, that gadget . . . *(She points to the recorder.) —does it work?—was used a lot. Although generally the people didn't know when they* were using it . . . Now you can tell me what you're going to do and why you're here. We can talk freely and no one on the corner will be watching, right? And they won't search the house after you've left, will they? At any rate, what can I hide now? I can say whether I'm for or against, can't I? Right now, if I want, I can talk against the new government and nothing'll happen. It's possible. Is it possible? . . . Yes, everything's like that. Right there, on the corner, they sold beer today. There was noise. *Music* they call it. People don't look so messy anymore, or so angry. The trees no longer have political slogans tacked on them. People stroll by. I see them. If you are sad, you don't have to pretend you aren't, if you know what I mean . . . People eat, hope, dream. Do people dream? . . . Bright clothing is seen everywhere. But I'm skeptical. I already told you; I'm poisoned. I know. I saw.

SCREEN: Face of the old woman that says, "I know. I saw." *(The screen becomes dark.)*

OLD WOMAN: Well, we have to get to the point, for that's what interests you. Now, one can't waste time. One works now, right? Before, the important thing to do was to fake it. One hopes . . . History's simple, I tell you. But, anyhow, these are things that you're not going to understand. Or almost anyone else these days. These are things that one cannot understand if one hasn't gone through them, like everything . . . He wrote a couple of books that should still be around, or maybe not. Perhaps right after the overthrow of the system, they burned them. Then, at the very beginning, of course, they did those things. Inherited vices. It's been so hard, how well I know, to overcome those "tendencies"—is that what they're called still? All those books, you know, spoke well of the ousted system. And nonetheless, all they said was a bunch of lies. If he had to go out to the countryside, he went. No one ever knew that the more furiously he worked, the more he hated the system. He didn't do it out of devotion, but out of hate. You had to see with what passion he scratched the earth, how he sowed, weeded, and spaded. At that time those things were big plus points. Jesus! And with what hate he did everything, with what hate he cooperated in everything. He loathed all of it!

SCREEN: Quick view of an escorted man, a frenzied crowd, shouts of "Paredón!" *(The screen becomes dark.)*

OLD WOMAN: They made him a . . . he became a "model youth," "first-class worker." He was awarded the "prize." If someone had to do an extra turn at guard, he'd do it. If it was necessary to go to the sugar fields to cut sugar cane, he'd go. In the military service, what could he refuse to do if everything was official, patriotic, revolutionary, that is, essential? And outside of the military duty, everything else was also compulsory service, all the harder for him because by then he was no longer a boy. He was a man, and he had to live, that is, he needed a room, a pressure cooker, an extra pair of pants. You wouldn't believe me if I told you that the issuance of a coupon to buy a shirt involved a political privilege. I can see you don't believe me. What are we going to do with you? . . . May you always be the way you are . . .

SCREEN: Rapid view of an aroused crowd, parades, cries of, "Whoever sticks his head out, we'll cut it off." *(The screen becomes dark.)*

OLD WOMAN: . . . Since he hated the system so much, he limited himself to saying little. Since he didn't talk, he didn't contradict himself like the rest who had to correct or deny what they said today the next day—problems of "dialectics" they said. And, since he didn't contradict himself, he became a man of trust, of respect. In the weekly meetings, he never interrupted. You had to see the expression of agreement on his face, while in his mind he sailed, traveled, dreamed he was someplace else, in "enemy lands"—as they used to say. He dreamed that he came back in a plane with a bomb, and that right there in the meeting where he was, in the square full of slaves, where so many times he had hopelessly attended gatherings and applauded, he'd let it fall.

SCREEN: Rapid view of Revolution Square. Parade of tanks. Voice off stage: "Commander in Chief, the troops are in perfect formation and await your inspection." *(The screen becomes dark.)*

OLD WOMAN: . . . So that, "because of his discipline and attention in the Study Circles"—that's what they called the mandatory political indoctrination classes—he got still another diploma . . . . When it came time to read the Granma[3]—I still remember that title—he was the first in line, not because the paper interested him, but because he loathed it so much that in order to get it over with quickly—the way one wants to get rid of anything one detests—he read it immediately. When he'd raise his hand to donate this, that, whatever—we used to donate everything publicly—how he laughed to himself, how he exploded inside. He'd always do four or five extra hours of work, "voluntary hours," but what would have happened if he hadn't done them?

. . . During the compulsory guard duty, with his rifle on his shoulder, he'd walk through the building the previous regime had built, watching over his own hell. How often he thought of blowing out his brains while shouting "down with the dictatorship," or something like that. But life's different. People are different. Do you know what fear is? Do you know what hate is? Do you know what hope is? Do you know what impotence is? Take care of yourself. Don't trust; don't trust anyone. Not even now, even less now. Today when everything encourages confidence is the right time to distrust. Later it'll be too late. Afterward you'll have to obey. You're young. You don't know anything. However, your father was probably a militiaman. Without a doubt your father . . . *(She stares at the journalist who, as though upset, makes a gesture of negation.)* Your father, no doubt . . . *(Pause.)* Don't take part in anything! Leave the country! Can one leave now? It's unbelievable, leaving . . . *(She gets up and walks around the journalist.)* "If I could leave," he used to tell me. He'd whisper it to me after returning from another endless day, after having spent three hours applauding. "If I could leave, if I only could, swimming, anything else's impossible—escape from this hell and get lost." And I, "Calm down, calm down. You know darn well it's impossible. Fishermen bring back pieces of fingers. What if you try and you're caught? They have orders to shoot at close range on the high sea. Look at those lights . . . " Sometimes he himself had to take care of the lights and the guns—clean them, polish them, check over the objects of his subjection. *(She walks until she remains next to the screen, her back turned.)* And with how much discipline he did it! And with what passion! One'd say it was a matter of his real self not showing through these acts. And he'd come back home, beat, dirty, covered with awards . . . "Ah, if I had a bomb," he'd say to me then, or rather he'd whisper to me, "I'd have already blown up all of this. A powerful bomb that'd leave nothing, not even me." And I . . .

SCREEN: As soon as the old woman says, "And I," the screen is illuminated. The character of the old woman appears on it, but thirty years younger, saying, "Calm down. For God's sake, wait. Don't say any more. They can hear you. Don't ruin it all with your anger . . ." *(The screen becomes dark.)*

OLD WOMAN: *(Now at stage center.)* And I, "Calm down. For God's sake, wait. Don't say any more. They can hear you. Don't ruin it all with your anger . . . "

SCREEN: Documentary. Thousands of arms waving machetes. Voice off stage, stentorian, threatening: CHARGE! DEATH TO THE TRAITORS! *(The screen becomes dark.)*

OLD WOMAN: . . . Disciplined, courteous, hardworking, discrete, plain, normal, natural, absolutely natural, adaptive, precisely for being the exact opposite. Why wouldn't they make him a member of the party? What task wouldn't he do? And quickly! What criticism wouldn't he accept humbly? . . . And that enormous hate inside of him, that feeling of being harassed, annihilated, buried, unable to say a word. And he took all that, quietly, how quietly! Enthusiastically! So as not to be more harassed, annihilated, absolutely damned. Just in order to be himself one day perhaps, to take revenge: to speak, to act, to live . . .

SCREEN: *(Interrupting the old woman.)* Inflamed crowd. Documentary of an official Cuban parade in front of the Peruvian embassy in Havana. Authoritarian voice off stage, "My home, clean and pretty, without idlers or fairies." *(The screen becomes dark.)*

OLD WOMAN: . . . Ah, how he wept ever so softly at night in his room. There, in that room, the one on this side . . . he cried out of anger and hate. I could never list, even if I were to live for that alone, the insults he said against the regime. "I can't go on, I can't go on," he'd say to me. And it was true. His arms were around me, embracing me. I was also young then. We were young, like you. Although, maybe not, you're not so young. Today everyone's well fed. Embracing me he'd say, "I'm not going to be able to go on. I won't be able to go on. I'm going to scream all my hate. I'm going to shout out all my hate," he'd whisper to me, suffocating. And I, what would I do? I'd quiet him. I'd say to him:

SCREEN: Close up of the old woman, thirty years younger, saying, "Are you crazy?" *(The screen becomes dark.)*

OLD WOMAN: And I'd straighten up his medals . . .

SCREEN: *(Figure of the old woman, thirty years younger.)* "If you do, they're going to shoot you. Pretend like everyone else. Pretend more than the next guy, that way you'll make fun of them. Calm down. Don't say anything foolish . . . " *(The screen becomes dark.)*

OLD WOMAN: He kept on doing his job. Sometimes, at night, he was his own self when he came to me to get things off his chest. Not even now, when one is encouraged to put down the overthrown regime, have I heard anyone speak so badly of that system. Since he worked in it, he knew the system, its most subtle atrocities . . . During the day he'd return infuriated and silent to guard duty, the assembly, the field, the raised fist. He was loaded with "awards" . . . It was then that the party *persuaded* him—you don't know what that verb meant in those days—to write a series of biographies of its highest leaders. "Do it! Do it!," I told him, "or everything you've gotten up to now'll be lost. It'd be the end." He became . . . they made him famous.

SCREEN: Fidel Castro appears, pinning medals on a group of people. Silent projection while the old woman keeps on talking.

OLD WOMAN: He moved away from here. They gave him a big house. He got married to the woman they suggested he marry. I had a sister living in exile . . . *(The screen becomes dark.)* He had a son . . . *(Pause.)* But he continued to visit me, though watching, hoping not to be seen when he came here. He'd come with his books, his biographies under his arms. He'd give them to me and tell me the truth about the biographees, every one of whom was a monster. *(She stops at stage center and looks directly at the audience.)* Were they? Or were we all?

SCREEN: Close up of the old woman who asks, "Were they? Or were we all?" *(The screen becomes dark.)*

OLD WOMAN: *(To the journalist.)* What do you think? Did you learn something about *your father*? Have you learned anything? What more do you want to know? . . . Why are you interviewing me? Why are you looking at me that way? Who are you? Why did you choose so troubled a person for your work? What do you know about him? . . .

SCREEN: Infuriated crowd. Cries of "Paredón!" *(The screen becomes dark.)*

OLD WOMAN: "The first chance I have, I'll seek asylum," he'd tell me. "I know there's a lot of surveillance, that it's practically impossible to defect. The spies and executioners are all over. Later, in exile, I'll be assassinated. But before that, I'll speak out; I'll say what I think and tell the truth." "Calm down, calm down," I'd tell him. We weren't so young then. "Don't do anything foolish . . . " And he, "Do you think I can spend all my life pretending? Don't you realize that by betraying myself to this degree, I'm going to stop being me? Don't you see I'm a shadow, a puppet, an actor who never comes down off the stage where he plays a dirty role? . . . " And I'd say, "Wait, wait . . . " understanding, weeping with him too, hating as much or more than he, pretending like everybody else, secretly conspiring with my thought, my soul, and begging him to wait, to wait. And he knew how to wait. Until the moment came. *(Pause. Total illumination.)* The moment when the regime was overthrown, and he was accused and condemned as a direct agent of the tyranny. All the evidence was against him, and he was condemned to the maximum penalty, death by shooting. Then, standing before the firing squad that'd shoot him, he shouted, "Down with Castro! Long live liberty! . . . " He kept on shouting until the heavy fire silenced him. Cries that the press and the world called *cowardly cynicism*, but that I—write it down in case that gadget doesn't work—can assure you, were the only authentic thing he said aloud in his entire life.

The lights around the old woman are turned off. The screen is illuminated by a light that becomes more and more intense without projecting any image, only a blinding and dazzling light. Suddenly, a total darkness. From within that darkness, off stage, the voice of the old woman is heard saying, "I know. I saw." Silence. Darkness.)

CURTAIN

Notes

[1]As used here, militiaman refers to the Cuban civilian militia rather than to an actual member of the armed forces.

[2]*Paredón*, the wall against which prisoners are placed to be shot. The expression here is the equivalent of *Kill him.*

[3]Official newspaper of the Castro government.

Screens

Dolores Prida

Dolores Prida

Dolores Prida was born in Caibarién, province of Las Villas, in 1943. She received her elementary education and attended business school there. In 1960 her father left Cuba illegally by boat. The following year Prida left the island with the rest of her family and settled in New York City. Between 1963 and 1966 she took courses in literature at Hunter College. Since 1969 she has held several important positions, among them: international correspondent for Collier-MacMillan International (1969-70); Director of Information Services of the National Puerto Rican Forum (1971-73); Arts and Science Editor and New York correspondent of *Visión, The Latin American Magazine* (1977-80); and Literary Manager at INTAR (International Arts Relations, Inc.) Hispanic American Theater (1980-83). She is now Director of Publications at the Association of Hispanic Arts (1983 to the present.)

Prida has published several plays and two books of poetry, as well as short stories and poems in numerous American and international journals. She has received several grants and awards: Cintas Literature Fellowship, 1976; CAPS (Community Arts Program Services of the New York State Council of the Arts) Playwriting Fellowship, 1979-80; and INTAR Playwright-in-Residence, 1982-83. She has also spoken at a variety of theatrical and academic conferences and symposia.

To date, Dolores Prida has written eight plays, all of which have been widely staged in the United States and some abroad. Her plays include *Beautiful Señoritas* (1977), *The Beggars Soap Opera* (1979), *La era latina* (1980), *Coser y cantar* (1981), *Crisp!* (1981), *Juan Bobo* (1981), *Savings* (1985), and *Pantallas* (1986-87), included here, her first play written totally in Spanish.

The action in *Pantallas* takes place during a period when much of the world is in danger of being destroyed by an unspecified nuclear attack or accident. The characters, who are so immersed in themselves they cannot see—or do not wish to see—the truth of the situation, do not accept fully their imminent destruction. They are, according to the author, representative of many Latin Americans, who are victims of "cultural alienation and lack of information fostered by the television medium."

These characters (three soap opera actors, one female and two male) rehearse and improvise scenes that could become scripts for future soaps when the world returns to "normal" and the television stations that have already ceased to transmit, start operating again. Throughout the entire play Prida exploits in a sustained and masterful manner the technique of "theater within the theater." The drama never allows the spectators to know for a fact whether what they observe is a game the actors play or whether they act moved by their own reality. Although too many hints point to the final annihilation, the intermingling of fiction and reality creates an ambiguity which enriches this work on many levels.

Screens

Characters

ELENA, a soap actress, in her late forties. She has a faded beauty and an air of resignation about it, although she holds on to the memories of her past fame.

ROBERTO, a soap actor, in his late forties or early fifties. He is tall and handsome, somewhat disillusioned with life and with his profession.

MAURICIO, a soap actor, twenty-two. Young and strikingly handsome. He is full of hopes concerning life and the future of his acting career.

Setting

The only setting is the living room of a beach cottage in a Caribbean country. It is furnished modestly, but in good taste, with an assortment of tropical styles.

At stage right there is a sofa and coffee table. Next to the sofa a higher table with a telephone. Stage left, a bar with two high stools, glasses, bottles, and a small television set. Rear center stage a large window with Venetian blinds, which remain closed throughout the action. Behind the bar and to the left of it, there is a door leading to another room of the house.

The entire play takes place during the same day, in the near future. Perhaps tomorrow. Hopefully never.

Production Notes

1. The songs included in the play are literal translations of popular

Hispanic songs. They can be substituted for actual lyrics of well-known American songs with similar meaning.

2. In the speech where soap opera stars are mentioned, their names can be changed to those of stars popular at the moment of production.

As the lights go up Elena and Mauricio are seated on the sofa kissing passionately. Suddenly, Roberto enters.

ROBERTO: That's how I wanted to catch you! I'd suspected that something was going on between the two of you for quite some time. I had a feeling in my gut, a constant, painful sensation that wouldn't let me sleep. *(Pulls out a gun.)* But it's all over now. Tonight I'll sleep in peace! *(He aims the gun at Mauricio and Elena, but his hand begins to shake. Roberto lowers the gun and places his other hand on his head, talking to himself.)* What am I doing? This whole thing's ridiculous. A modern husband wouldn't act this way. *(To Elena and Mauricio.)* Forget it. Carry on.

Roberto exits. Elena and Mauricio, who had been petrified by fear, sigh with relief, look at each other, smile, and begin kissing again. Roberto enters once more. He looks at the scene, somewhat surprised, but recovers quickly without getting upset. He smiles, loosening his tie.

ROBERTO: Dear . . . Mauricio . . . How are you? Hot today, isn't it? *(He goes to the bar, pours three drinks, and brings them to the sofa. He sits next to Elena, who now is sandwiched between the two men.)*

ELENA: *(Embarrassed.)* Roberto, darling, I didn't know you were coming home early today. I thought . . .

ROBERTO: Forgive me for not letting you know I'd be home early. I'm sorry for the inconvenience, dear. *(Placing a hand on Mauricio's knee.)* And how are you doing, Mauricio, old pal?

MAURICIO: *(Embarrassed.)* Fine, just fine. I was just telling Elena here that . . .

ROBERTO: *(Calmly.)* Let's stop fooling one another, shall we? I know quite well what you were up to. I'm not stupid. Look, for some time now I've known what was going on between you two. I couldn't get rid of the thought . . . it was like a toothache.

ELENA: Roberto, my love, forgive me! This is the first time. You know very well. In twelve years of marriage I've never been unfaithful to you!

MAURICIO: It happened suddenly, unexpectedly. It was just a moment of madness . . .

ROBERTO: *(Stands up, calmly.)* You know I'm going to kill the two of you, don't you? I have no choice. My honor is at stake. *(He draws the gun.)*

ELENA: *(Falling to her knees, screaming melodramatically.)* Please, my love, don't do it! Think of our children!

ROBERTO: But . . . we don't have children!

ELENA: I know, but if you kill me we'll never have any.

MAURICIO: *(Standing up and stepping out of character.)* I don't like this at all.

ELENA: Neither do I.

ROBERTO: You're right. It's somewhat trite.

MAURICIO: The love triangle, the infidelity touch, all that's fine. The audience'll go for that. Deceit is always appealing . . . But, I don't know, I think we could be more original.

ROBERTO: Yes, we could. Also, I shouldn't pull out the gun at that point.

ELENA: Not only that . . . You can't kill me just like that, so soon. We agreed that the three roles would be equally important and that no one would be terminated until the last episode.

ROBERTO: Right. That was the agreement. It was just an idea.

ELENA: Well, that idea didn't work.

ROBERTO: OK. Let's try something else.

MAURICIO: I don't know if this is the best way to go about it. Perhaps we should discuss the idea first, think about the situation before we start to . . .

ELENA: I agree. We should be more methodic and study themes, characters, time, place, and setting before we start improvising scenes.

ROBERTO: I don't think that's necessary. We've played in dozens of soaps. Don't you think that by now we know what works and what doesn't work?

MAURICIO: Forgive me, but, with all due respect for your experience, it seems to me that getting a good writer to develop the script for us would be the wisest thing to do. After all, we're actors, not writers.

ROBERTO: Good writers don't want to waste time with soaps.

ELENA: Besides, there's no money in it for them . . .

ROBERTO: And they want to make the stories too serious or too intellectual.

ELENA: Believe me, we don't need a writer.

ROBERTO: Anyhow, at a time like this, where could we find a scriptwriter?

ELENA: Don't worry, we've plenty of time to develop our own script.

MAURICIO: You're right. We'll be better off writing it ourselves. We'll have absolute control over the roles we'll play. We'll write ourselves into each episode. We'll make more money . . .

ELENA: We'll become famous again. We'll be recognized in the streets, like before. People'll ask for our autographs in the supermarkets. We'll make TV specials, travel throughout Latin America, make records with the hit singers of the moment . . .

MAURICIO: Records? We're not singers!

ELENA: It doesn't matter. We'll be famous and fame works wonders. I can picture myself singing in Central Stadium before thirty thousand people . . . *(Singing.)*

> Something within me, something within me
> is beginning to die, and I . . .
> I want to live, I want to live . . .[1]

MAURICIO: *(Excited.)* Women'll faint when I walk onto the stage! They'll rip off their clothes shouting my name: Mau-ri-cio, Mau-ri-cio!

ROBERTO: I'll be satisfied with getting a fat check for doing what I like best: acting.

ELENA: You'll never amount to anything! You always think small. You're satisfied with life's common petty rewards. In life, my dear, one must think big, reach higher.

ROBERTO: We're wasting our time with these childish fantasies. Let's try something else . . . another idea.

ELENA: That's it, ideas, great ideas, right? Always in search of ideas, *other people's ideas*. You are a brain leech. You never come up with an idea of your own . . . although one must give you credit for your skill in appropriating other people's ideas, passing them off as your own, making money on them. Do you realize your success is due to other people's ideas? Aren't you ashamed? Don't you feel . . . cheap?

ROBERTO: Not at all, darling. That's my line: ideas, taken from whomever. There are many who have extraordinary ideas, but don't do anything with them. Those people can simply go to hell! As for you, dear, you shouldn't complain. You enjoy quite a comfortable life-style thanks to those very ideas I . . . borrow.

ELENA: *(Sarcastic laugh.)* Ha, ha. Comfortable, true. Quite comfortable. A mansion in an exclusive neighborhood, ten maids, three cars, my personal hairdresser, mink coats, trips to Europe . . . Yes, darling, I live like a queen, but the one thing your borrowed ideas have not been able to give me is . . . happiness . . .

ROBERTO: That's been your great mistake, María Eugenia de la Campa, waiting for others to make you happy. Did it ever occur to you to work on your own happiness?

ELENA: Yes, it has. I've masturbated on numerous occasions, but . . .

MAURICIO: *(Suddenly interrupting.)* Cut! Cut!

ROBERTO: But why? It was going so well . . .

ELENA: Wasn't I terrific?

MAURICIO: Are you morons or what? You know you can't say *masturbate* on TV!

ELENA: Why not?

MAURICIO: "Why not?" Have you ever heard Joan Collins say "masturbate?" Have you ever heard Victoria Principal say "masturbate?" Or Linda Evans, have you ever heard her say such a word?

ELENA: *(Thinking.)* Well, no . . . not on television . . .

ROBERTO: OK, fine. You made your point. We can't use "contemporary" language. We have to be more careful . . . more "classical."

MAURICIO: Classical . . . hmmm . . . *(He walks around thinking.)* Classical . . . That's it, classical! With a classic we can't miss.

ELENA: For heaven's sake! Classics are fine for the theater, but TV has to be modern.

MAURICIO: I don't mean a true classical play, but an adaptation. We place the action in a present day setting and . . . presto! We have a hit.

ROBERTO: Oh? For instance?

MAURICIO: Let me see . . . *(He thinks.)* A universal story, something one could still relate to nowadays. Something like . . . *Don Juan Tenorio.*

ELENA: You're kidding. In this day and age? Honey, since Women's Lib Don Juan is obsolete, passé, gone.

ROBERTO: Passé? I don't know where you've been. There are Don Juans in action everywhere, every day. *(With a Don Juanesque air.)* I know what I'm talking about.

MAURICIO: *(Very enthused.)* Yes, yes. Let's try a scene. How about the one with Don Luis and Don Juan at the inn?

ELENA: Hold it right there!

ROBERTO: What is it?

ELENA: Doña Inés is not in that scene.

ROBERTO: That's . . . true.

MAURICIO: She comes in later on. In this scene you can do something else.

ELENA: Like what?

MAURICIO: You can be . . . the waitress.

ELENA: Waitress, my foot! I want to start playing Doña Inés from the start.

ROBERTO: *(Impatient.)* OK, OK, do whatever you want!

Elena puts a white piece of cloth on her head and ties it under her chin in order to look like a nun. She stands behind the bar. Mauricio will play Don Luis and Roberto will play Don Juan. Roberto sits on a bar stool. Elena pours him a drink. Mauricio enters as Don Luis.

MAURICIO: Greetings, my lord . . .

ROBERTO: *(Stepping out of character.)* That's the wrong start.

MAURICIO: Why?

ROBERTO: No one says "Greetings, my lord" nowadays.

MAURICIO: You're right. Let's try it again.

They start the scene once more.

MAURICIO: Hi 'ya there, bro', panita!

ROBERTO: *(Stepping out of character, with contained exasperation.)* Excuse me, Mauricio, but that "panita" business . . . We haven't discussed whether this is going to be a Puerto Rican adaptation or what. Only Puerto Ricans understand what panita means. I think our adaptation has to have a more universal appeal. We can't limit our market.

MAURICIO: What do you want, then? Should we speak like "proper" Spaniards and lisp all over the TV cameras?

ROBERTO: That's not what I'm saying. What I mean is . . .

ELENA: *(Interrupting them, exasperated.)* Shit! This is just an improvisation! Let him use whatever fucking language he wants! *(Realizing she's playing a nun, she crosses herself.)*

MAURICIO: Doña Inés is right.

ROBERTO: OK. Let's get on with it.

They start the scene once more.

MAURICIO: So, here you are, Juan Tenorio. I see you've kept our appointment.

ROBERTO: I'm a man of my word. A year ago we agreed to meet in this tavern to settle a bet, and here I am. What would you like to drink?

MAURICIO: A Heineken.

ROBERTO: *(Stepping out of character.)* A Heineken! A Heineken? Don Luis would never ask for a Heineken!

ELENA: *(Interrupting, eager to continue the scene.)* Why not? Here's your Heineken, sir. *(She bangs the bottle on the counter.)* Proceed, please.

MAURICIO: *(Winking at Elena.)* Thank you, Doña.

Roberto stands up, suddenly furious.

ROBERTO: "Thank you, Doña," "Thank you, Doña." That's so ridiculous! Anyone watching us through a keyhole'd think we're insane! Perhaps we are—the effect of radiation on our brains!

Roberto walks to the TV set and turns it on with a blow of his hand. There's nothing, only a snowy picture.

ELENA: Leave that TV alone. You know darn well there isn't a single channel broadcasting for the time being.

ROBERTO: For the time being? They'll never broadcast again! Can't you understand that? Never again will there be any soaps. We're wasting our time. As a matter of fact, we've already wasted all of it.

MAURICIO: *(Dead serious.)* We had agreed not to bring the subject up ever again. You give too much importance to the whole thing. The networks will be on the air again. Soon. There'll be hundreds of new soaps and we'll be the stars. When things get sorted out, producers will need new scripts and we'll be there, ready for them.

ELENA: *(Takes the cloth off her head, goes to the TV set and turns it off.)*

Let's rest a while. We've been at this too long. There's no need to rush.

Roberto goes to the window, peeks through the blind. Mauricio sits on the sofa, holding his head in his hands. Elena looks into her purse.

ELENA: Dammit! I'm out of cigarettes.

ROBERTO: *(Turning toward Elena and looking at her while shaking his head in disbelief.)* Imagine. The end of the world and nothing to smoke.

MAURICIO: *(Raising his head without moving.)* There's some grass in the icebox, in the mustard jar.

ELENA: No, what I want is an ordinary cigarette.

ROBERTO: Nothing is ordinary any longer. Now everything is *special.*

ELENA: Don't start with your cheap philosophy. I'm going to take a shower. We'll continue with the script later.

Elena exits. Roberto takes a small portable cassette player from the table, puts on the earphones and listens for a while.

ROBERTO: *This* is a real crisis! We've only one cassette and it's Julio Iglesias.

MAURICIO: Elena forgot to bring the cassette case.

ROBERTO: *(Taking off the earphones.)* I don't know why you invited her. The beach house was lent *to me*, and I invited *you*. My idea was to spend a few quiet days . . . and look how it all ended up.

MAURICIO: She's not to blame for what's happening . . . out there.

ROBERTO: We're all to blame for what's happening out there . . . but, so what? There's nothing we can do about it now. I would have preferred her not to come.

MAURICIO: Your invitation was sort of vague, Roberto. You should have warned me that the invitation was for me alone. You know I've been going with Elena since we did "In the Open" together. I had no idea her presence annoyed you so much.

ROBERTO: It's not that . . . Elena and I have known each other for ages. Certain things happened between us . . . which I'd rather not talk about.

Elena enters frightened and pale.

ELENA: There's no water!

MAURICIO: What do you mean "there's no water"?

ELENA: There's no water . . . not a drop.
MAURICIO: Can't be!

Mauricio runs into another room. Roberto goes to the bar and calmly pours himself a drink.

ROBERTO: I don't know what you'd expect.

Mauricio enters frightened and pale.

MAURICIO: There's no water. Not a single drop. We'll die of thirst.
ELENA: . . . and stinking too!
ROBERTO: *(Taking a sip from his drink.)* There are three bottles of rum, one of whisky, half a bottle of tequila, some vodka, and one of gin that hasn't even been opened.

Elena, on the verge of hysteria, grabs the glass from Roberto's hand and smashes it against the wall.

ELENA: I'm fed up with your jokes. And I'm sick and tired of your air of superiority, of your calmness, and your sanity. It isn't the moment for any of that!

Elena leaves, furious. Mauricio drags himself to the sofa like a thirsty man lost in the desert.

MAURICIO: Water . . . water . . . There's no water. Not a drop. I'm dying of thirst. My throat's dry. I'd give anything . . . anything for a glass of cold water . . . so cold it'd make my teeth numb. A glass of cold water . . . I can see it . . . It must be a mirage . . . The glass is sweating, with ice cubes floating in the crystal clear liquid, the cubes tinkling against the sides of the glass *(He swallows.)* . . . Water, what a wonderful, simple, humble, refreshing thing . . . a glass of water . . . I'm dying for a glass of water. *(He sticks out his tongue and touches his throat with both hands.)*
ROBERTO: You never used to drink water before. You belonged to the "Pepsi Generation." Remember? You even drank the stuff for breakfast.
MAURICIO: *(Stepping out of character.)* You don't have to insult me! Things change, people change. Now I'm dying for a glass of water.

Elena enters in a wheelchair, her hair wrapped in a towel resembling a turban. She is wearing a dressing gown. She moves the wheelchair to the middle of the room.

ELENA: *(In a mesmerizing voice.)* Mauricio.

MAURICIO: *(Turning toward her, mesmerized.)* At your service, madam.

ELENA: Come here. *(Mauricio approaches her.)* On your knees. *(Mauricio kneels. She hands him a jar of cream.)* Rub cream on my feet . . . *(Sighing with pleasure.)* . . . María just gave me a bath that has truly revived me.

Mauricio rubs cream on her feet and stares at them, fascinated.

MAURICIO: Madam . . . may I kiss your foot?

ELENA: You may kiss it, my child. *(Sighs.)* Oh, how many famous lips have kissed that foot. That was before my accident . . . of course . . . when I was the highest paid ballerina in the world. Princes from Saudi Arabia, prime ministers, international bankers, shipping tycoons, violinists . . .

MAURICIO: And now my lips, the lips of a simple illiterate servant . . . *(He kisses her foot.)*

ROBERTO: *(From the bar as he pours himself another drink.)* I remember that one: "The Cripple's Waltz." A hundred and sixty episodes. At the top of the ratings for three years. I played the role of Renato. How could I forget? It was our first soap together.

Mauricio stands up, goes to the bar, sits on a stool, and pours himself a drink.

MAURICIO: I didn't miss a single episode. I was still a child, but my mother watched it every day. *(Mauricio shakes slightly. He rubs his bare arms.)* Aren't you cold?

ELENA: It's August.

ROBERTO: That was before . . . August, September, October.

MAURICIO: I'll get a sweater.

Mauricio goes to the bedroom. Roberto looks at Elena who is still sitting in the wheelchair. He approaches her, stands behind her, puts his hands on her shoulders, speaking with great sincerity.

ROBERTO: I fell in love with you when I saw you in that wheelchair . . . For the first time you looked different to me, vulnerable. I felt that perhaps you could need me . . . that perhaps there was something I could give you. You had been so arrogant, so self-sufficient . . . the unreachable star was now within my reach . . . I almost believed it . . . Sometimes you were so sincere, so real. I remember the night I invited you to listen to my collection of old records. I played an old corny bolero, one of those heard at corner bar jukeboxes. I said to you: "I don't know if you'll like these oldies . . . " And you answered: "They're not just oldies . . . they're anthems. . . . " I fell in love with you even more.

Elena moves her wheelchair forward a short distance away from Roberto. She speaks without looking at him.

ELENA: Perhaps what you felt was pity; a beautiful and famous woman confined to a wheelchair has a special attraction. But I don't want that kind of love, Renato. I prefer to be alone, to live on memories, on my past glory. I sit here and relive in my mind my most glorious moments . . . the performance of *Swan Lake* I gave in Paris . . . *Les Sylphides* in Milan. *(She moves the wheelchair closer to the window.)* Forgive me, Renato, but you have to understand that the simple love of a man like you can't compete with my legendary past. It's best for you to forget me.

They look briefly at each other. Mauricio enters and looks at Elena, then at Roberto. Elena exits in her wheelchair. Mauricio is wearing a sweatshirt and a towel around his neck. Roberto pours drinks for himself and Mauricio.

ROBERTO: Here! Join me for a drink. Let's see if one can really drown one's sorrows in booze. To tell the truth, I've never been able to do it. My sorrows seem to be Olympic swimmers.

MAURICIO: I don't know if you can drown anything in alcohol, but at least it warms your insides. I'm so cold! . . . Why is it so cold? Whatever happened to our tropical summer?

ROBERTO: Forget all that . . . none of it matters . . . at all. The coldness I feel in my soul is much greater. *(Half drunk.)* Mauri . . . Women are castrating bitches. Do you realize what us men have to go through on account of them? The only worthwhile woman in a man's life is his own mother. The only one. The rest are harpies, torturers, ball-busters.

MAURICIO: They screw up our lives; they ruin us. What's left?

ROBERTO: Friends, your pals . . . that's what's left. Listen . . . I

. . . I gave up a life of wine, women, and song; I gave up my drinking buddies because she asked me. I became an honest man, hardworking, responsible . . . And for what? For nothing. She left me for a rich man; an old, fat millionaire . . . Can you believe that?

MAURICIO: I can believe anything of a woman. Look, it's the best thing that could have happened to you. *(Raising his glass.)* Let's toast to female betrayal!

They raise their glasses and drink. Roberto puts his arm around Mauricio. They sing.

MAURICIO AND ROBERTO:

"Many years of illusion passed
enjoying the delights of my sweet love,
but in the end I came to understand
that any friend is worthier,
even if he's a drunkard or a sinner,
than the most beautiful woman."[2]

During the song Roberto has moved in closer to Mauricio, singing in his ear, insinuatingly. Elena enters and catches them in this position. Roberto quickly moves away. Elena goes to the window and looks through the slats.

ELENA: It's very windy on the beach. The waves are so big; it's scary just to watch.

She moves away from the window. Goes over to the couch and sits on it.

ROBERTO: I don't know how you can see in the dark. We've been in total darkness for three days now. Three days without the sun . . . Don't you miss it?

Elena looks through some books and newspapers lying on the coffee table.

ELENA: I've never liked the sun. It isn't good for you, you know. It gives you freckles. And wrinkles . . . it can give you skin cancer. Who needs it? *(Throwing back a book contemptuously.)* There's nothing to read in this house!

ROBERTO: And what are those? Pork chops for dinner?

MAURICIO: They could very well be. There's hardly any food left.

ELENA: I mean some light reading . . . like . . . the *TV Guide*, *People*, *Cosmopolitan* . . .

ROBERTO: The owner of this house didn't read any of that stuff. He was an educated man, very well informed on the issues of our time. That's why, when the crisis started, he took the first plane out to New Zealand. He thought he'd have a better chance there.

MAURICIO: *(Uncomfortable.)* There you go again.

ROBERTO: *(Sarcastic.)* If you don't want to hear about it, why don't you go take a walk, or go down to the beach for a swim, or take a nap under a coconut tree? Go on . . . go.

ELENA: And what about you? Why don't you make an appointment with your exorcist?

Roberto goes to the phone and dials a number.

ROBERTO: Hello! Hello! . . . May I speak to Father Anthony, please. Hello! Hello! *(Ironic.)* Funny . . . the phone doesn't work. How very strange, there's no water either!

Elena brusquely grabs the phone away from Roberto.

ELENA: What do you mean "it doesn't work"? Of course it works. *(She presses the switch to get a dial tone, then dials a number.)* Of course it works . . . you'll see. It's ringing . . . Hello! Mrs. Rosello? . . . Do you know who this is? No? I am . . . I am "the other woman." Ha, ha, ha . . . I'm calling to tell you that Mauricio is going away with me. I'm the one he loves. He *adores* me, understand? . . . *(She listens.)* That? . . . That doesn't matter. Age is no problem when two people love each other the way we do. He may be younger than I, but I can give him those things an innocent girl like you can't. *(Mauricio sits near her. She caresses his hair while she continues talking into the phone.)* Are you saying I'm bad? Well . . . I am. I've played that role many times. I specialize in villainesses . . . But, dear, don't you see? Good women never get anywhere. They just become fat, lonely, and frustrated . . . The possibility of my going to *hell* doesn't scare me because the years I've spent on this earth have been heaven . . . *(She listens, reacting with disgust.)* Suicide! Taking your life is a cowardly act and in extreme bad taste. But if you insist, I recommend sleeping pills. It's a less dramatic suicide, but much more hygienic.

She hangs up with a flourish. Roberto applauds. Elena smiles, pleased with her performance. Mauricio, intrigued, lifts the receiver and listens. He realizes there's no dial tone, which noticeably disturbs him. He hangs up.

ROBERTO: Brava, bravissima! "Autumn Love?"

ELENA: No. "Heartless Woman." Two hundred episodes.

ROBERTO: Ah, yes! I'd forgotten. You were really evil in that one . . .

ELENA: Yes, the dragon lady in heat, spitting fire through every pore.

MAURICIO: *(Trying to disguise his preoccupation.)* Elena, do you remember that producer friend of yours, that Cuban guy from Miami? He'd be a good contact. We should send the new script to him first.

ROBERTO: For what? In the U.S. they don't make Spanish soaps. There they only watch the crap we make here.

ELENA: How can you say a thing like that? We've made soaps here that can very well compete with "Dynasty." Masterpieces of the genre.

ROBERTO: *(Derogatory, pouring himself another drink.)* Ha!

ELENA: You mean to tell me that "The Beautiful Vixen," my best role ever, wasn't a masterpiece? And what about "Kill Me, But Don't Leave Me"? I won the Golden Palm Award for that . . . even though I played the role of the "good woman" in it, that's to say, the victim.

MAURICIO: I remember that one. It had a lot to do with my decision to become a TV actor. My mother also had a lot to do with that decision. As a child I was so cute that my mother used to say that my face had to be admired by the whole world . . . She named me Mauricio after the main character in "Woman Without a Past." Being a television actor is what I always dreamed of. You know, one feels admired, loved. One becomes a part of people's daily lives. One gets into their homes and helps them not to think about reality . . . and to forget the misery that surrounds them . . . Yes, one exists beyond oneself . . .

ELENA: You're so right! It's something very special. One gets to live different lives and to die dramatic and spectacular deaths.

ROBERTO: *(Mockingly.)* Quite different from real life, isn't it? In real life most lives and deaths are quite boring, routine, totally pedestrian, aren't they?

ELENA: *(With intensity.)* Roberto, do you think I don't realize that most soaps are stupid, that they amuse people with stories that have nothing to do with reality? I know that quite well. But, what do you want me to do? I don't have the energy needed to change the world . . . I also had dreams and hopes. Do you think that as an actress I haven't wanted to play important roles on the stage or in films, epic roles with profound messages that would enlighten mankind and make it *think*? Of course, I have. You're not the only one who studied Method Acting, dear. I studied too. I prepared myself, spending plenty of time and money on acting, voice, and body expression workshops. But opportunity never knocked on my door. This is what fate had reserved for me—soap operas, tacky melodramas for housewives—and I do them to the best of my ability, with dignity, with my chin up, turning my back on the past, on my dreams, on what might have been . . .

Silent pause. They look at one another.

ROBERTO: I don't recall from what soap that monologue is. *(He exits.)*

ELENA: *(With contained anger.)* God! If I had the guts, I'd kill him one of these days!

MAURICIO: Don't pay any attention. He's drunk too much.

ELENA: It's not the drinks he's had . . . He's embittered, frustrated. He always wanted to be someone other than himself. He has always considered himself better than the rest . . . a serious actor fallen on bad times, a legitimate stage actor reduced to playing on the boob tube.

MAURICIO: Don't be so harsh with him. I'm gonna see what's the matter with him.

Mauricio exits. Elena shouts after him.

ELENA: Go ahead! Run! Go, lick his wounds! Do you think I don't know what's going on between you two? I've been in show business too long not to see what's happening. It won't be the first time a man steals my husband . . . And it won't be the last! . . . I've gone through everything in life, through everything! I can manage alone very well. *(She calms down and walks through the room, passing her hands over the furniture and the walls as she passes by. She ends up in front of the mirror hanging on the wall over the television set.)* Alone . . . a lifetime of fleeting love affairs with the handsomest men . . . with the most coveted heartthrobs, evenings of champagne and dreams in the most exclusive night clubs . . . but in the end, alone! Only the mirror knows the truth . . . *(She begins to crouch until her face is reflected in the television screen.)* Who am I? . . . How old am I? . . . What's my name? Where am I going? What's the real color of my hair? . . . But nothing matters any more, nothing . . . now that . . . now that I am . . . blind!

Mauricio, who, unseen, had watched Elena go through her scene from the line "Who am I?" joins in.

MAURICIO: Mrs. . . . Carnevale?

Elena turns toward Mauricio, her arms extended in front of her in the fashion of a blind person.

ELENA: Who are you? What are you doing here?

MAURICIO: I've come to fix your TV set. Sorry it took so long, but we're very busy at the shop. Half the town is having problems with their sets . . . What seems to be the problem here?

Mauricio goes to the television set and turns it around to examine it.

ELENA: Your voice sounds so familiar! Let me touch your face to see . . . I mean, to feel . . . whether or not I know you. *(She feels Mauricio's face with both hands, then touches his neck and chest. Her hands stop at a medal hanging from a chain around his neck. She touches it with great interest. She opens her eyes and looks at it with curiosity, stepping out of character.)* Mauricio . . . where did you get this medal? I've never seen it before.

MAURICIO: I've no idea where it came from. I've worn it ever since I can remember. . . . The nuns in the orphanage where I grew up . . . made me promise never to take it off.

ELENA: *(Noticeably upset and nervous.)* No . . . It can't be! It's impossible . . . After so many years . . .

MAURICIO: Elena, what's the matter? Why are you so pale? Your hands are sweating . . . Have you seen a ghost?

ELENA: A ghost? Yes . . . A ghost from my past. Mauricio . . . I've something to confess. That . . . that medal you're wearing . . . is . . . is . . . mine!

MAURICIO: That's impossible! I've had it ever since I was a child. I didn't even know you then.

ELENA: Yes, you knew me. That medal's mine. I hung it around your neck before I abandoned you on the steps of the hospice one cold and rainy morning. That morning I almost died of sorrow for what I had just done . . . Mauricio, my son, will you ever be able to forgive me?

MAURICIO: *(Confused.)* Son? . . . Forgive you? . . . I don't know what you mean, Elena . . .

ELENA: Don't ever call me Elena again, I beg you. Call me by the name I've been wanting to hear from your lips for so many years . . . Mother!

MAURICIO: *(Joyfully.)* Mother!

They embrace. Roberto, wrapped in a bedsheet in the fashion of a Roman toga, enters. Halfway through his speech, Mauricio will put on the earphones so as not to listen to him.

ROBERTO: *(As a Shakespearean actor.)* Mother! Father! Brothers and sisters! "Lend me your ears. I come to bury Caesar, not to praise him. The evil that men do lives after them, the good is oft interred with their bones." All the world is a screen, and projected on it we see the soap of our times, chapter by chapter. Time is of the essence, my friends. We find ourselves at the edge of the precipice, in the very eye of the storm. We can no longer hope for better tomorrows. All we have is this day, the certainty of this fleeting and unique instant. It is now time to dismantle our tents, pack our weapons, and bid farewell. Some of us did our best to win this battle, to warn the world about the danger. But we only encountered indifference, ignorance, superstition, mistrust . . . It's too late for recriminations; they'd be useless. Let us march, then, toward extinction, like the great beasts of primeval times, like arrogant dinosaurs, proud in the knowledge that we're the greatest and most powerful creatures that ever inhabited the earth. Let us march, like lemmings, toward extermination once again, at peace with the knowledge that in a not too distant future our bones will be admired in museums and our disappearance will be the subject of doctoral dissertations. Let us crawl toward destruction, convinced that our existence has not been in vain and that our brief presence on this planet has had a purpose, despite the fact that in the history of the universe, it has been but one brief, shining, flickering moment . . .

Elena screams like a madwoman.

ELENA: *Stop it!* I can't take it anymore! This is a mad house! I won't listen to another word! Enough, ENOUGH! I'd rather die right now than to live in this nightmare with two dangerous lunatics. I want to kill myself. I'm going to slash my wrists! Give me something to slash my wrists with . . . a knife, a razor blade, a machete . . .

In a wild state she searches everywhere in the room, until she finds a pair of oversized scissors. She tries to cut her wrists by inserting her arm between the open blades of the scissors.

ROBERTO: Elena, what are you doing?! Give me those scissors!

Frightened, Mauricio and Roberto try to take the scissors away from Elena. She gets even more violent and begins to attack them with the scissors. Roberto falls on the sofa and covers his head with a sheet trying to protect himself from the attack, but she stabs him savagely. He screams and dies. Elena then runs all over the room after Mauricio.

ELENA: You too, you too, Prince of Night! You too, Pretty Face! You too!

MAURICIO: Elena: have you gone mad? Drop the scissors! It's only a game!

ELENA: No, it isn't! Nothing's a game anymore. Everything's a game now. Games are all we've got!

Elena catches up with Mauricio and stabs him in the back. Mauricio falls to the floor in slow motion. Elena kneels beside him and holds him on her lap.

ELENA: *(Gently, tearfully.)* Son . . . ? My son, can you hear me? I abandoned you in the hospice because I couldn't raise you as a true mother should. I was an actress, always traveling, living and dying on the dilapidated, dusty stages of small town theaters. What kind of a life was that for a beautiful little boy like you? Forgive me . . . Please forgive me. *(She cries.)*

MAURICIO: *(Opening his eyes and making a great effort to speak.)* Elena . . .

ELENA: Yes, son? My beloved son . . . I want to hear your last words. *(She puts her ear closer to his mouth.)*

MAURICIO: Stew.

ELENA: Stew . . . ?

MAURICIO: *(Standing up.)* Yes, too many different things mixed up in the same pot. And besides, too melodramatic. Don't you think so, Roberto?

ROBERTO: *(From under the sheets.)* I don't know why we always end up with the same shit.

ELENA: Pardon me, but I totally disagree. You can't deny that the scissors scene was rather original.

MAURICIO: Sure . . . I've only seen it a dozen times or so. But I must confess that for a moment you really scared me. I thought you had really cracked up.

ELENA: *(Proud.)* The truth is that I was magnificent, wasn't I? *(Pause.)* Well . . . what shall we do now?

ROBERTO: *(Still from under the sheets.)* I'm tired of this stupid game. I want to rest in peace and arise on the seventh day when the world's been remade.

Mauricio puts on the earphones.

ELENA: He's getting morbid again.

MAURICIO: Ignore him. Come, let's dance.

Mauricio and Elena share the earphones with their heads close together, dancing in silence for a while. Suddenly, Elena removes her earphone.

ELENA: Mauricio, you know what?

MAURICIO: *(Removing his earphone.)* What?

ELENA: Look, I'm fed up with the seriousness of soaps . . . So much crying and suffering and betraying. Why can't there be soaps with music . . . and comedy?

MAURICIO: Gee, I don't know. Maybe because no one has come up with them.

ELENA: How does this grab you: a soap-operetta, but with popular music. All the dialogue consists of popular boleros that fit the situation.

MAURICIO: For example . . . ?

ELENA: For example . . . *(She thinks, gets an idea and then sings.)* " . . . And how are you?"[3]

MAURICIO: *(Singing.)* "Me? . . . Couldn't be happier. And how are you?"

ELENA: *(Singing.)* "I'm happy to be in love."

MAURICIO: *(Singing.)* "How did it happen . . . ?"

ELENA: *(Singing.)* "I can't explain how it happened. Perhaps his eyes did it, perhaps his lips. Perhaps it was his hands, or perhaps the touch of his skin. Perhaps it was the impatience of waiting so long."

Mauricio laughs, applauding.

MAURICIO: I love it! Great! I like the idea! Roberto, Roberto, are you listening?

ROBERTO: *(From under the sheets.)* "Good-bye my friends, good-bye old pals; so much fun we used to have, but now I have to go away; it is my turn to say good-bye."

ELENA: *(Slinking under the sheet with Roberto. Singing.)* "This passionate heart is eager to love again . . . "[4]

ROBERTO: *(Singing.)* "Stop, don't touch me. Because of you I am tortured by memories of the past . . . "

Mauricio takes his shirt off and dives under the sheet too.

MAURICIO: *(Singing.)* "Kiss me and forget you've done it. I'll give you my life if only you ask . . . "

The three continue singing under the sheet. One after the other, they stop singing. Suggestive sensuous sounds are heard. The lights dim slowly until there is a complete blackout. In the dark, the sound of wind and surf are heard. When the lights go up, the three are sitting on the sofa, their bare shoulders above the sheet, sharing a marijuana cigarette.

MAURICIO: You know what I'd like to have right now? A pizza with pepperoni.

ELENA: I could eat a steak, medium rare, with onions and French fries.

MAURICIO: No, I think I'd rather have some beef stew on white rice, with green fried plantains on the side.

ELENA: And strawberries and cream for dessert.

MAURICIO: Hmm, hmm. Peaches in heavy syrup.

ELENA: Viennese coffee.

ROBERTO: I could eat a couple of pork chops.

ELENA: Aren't you a vegetarian?

ROBERTO: I am. But now that I know I'll never get to eat a pork chop again, I'd give an arm for one.

ELENA: In that case, wouldn't it be more sensible to eat something you've never eaten before like . . .

MAURICIO: Caviar, I've never eaten caviar.

ELENA: You haven't missed much. Too salty.

ROBERTO: You know, I hadn't thought of that . . .

MAURICIO: Of what?

ROBERTO: Of all the things I've never done. Play golf, for example. Never tried it.

ELENA: It's a sport for old people.

ROBERTO: I've never been to New York.

ELENA: I've never been to Japan.

ROBERTO: I've never climbed the Andes.

ELENA: I've never planted a tree.

ROBERTO: I've never swum in a river.

ELENA: I've never walked barefoot in the snow.

ROBERTO: I've never changed a baby's diapers.

ELENA: I've never had a baby.

ROBERTO: I've never . . .

Mauricio stands up very upset.

MAURICIO: I've never fished for marlin! I've never caught a butterfly! I've never built a wall with my own hands! You may not have done lots of things, but you've done much more than I have. I'm only twenty-two! I'm supposed to have a lifetime ahead of me. I still have to fall really in love, climb mountains, get my first gray hair. I haven't even read *One Hundred Years of Solitude* yet . . . Never! Never! I can't accept it, I just can't! It isn't fair that some old fart has pushed a button and everything's going to hell. Never! You know what I'll *never* be able to accept? The fact that the world is ruled by decrepit old men full of decrepit old ideas!

Elena gets up slowly. After some hesitation she goes to the TV set and turns it on. Static drowns Mauricio's last few words. It is very cold. The air has become noticeably polluted. Roberto turns the set off.

ROBERTO: Too strong, too realistic, Mauricio. You just can't display so much passion before the cameras. Besides, that was a very vague monologue. What exactly were you talking about? What's the source of your emotional explosion? No, I don't think we can use it.

Mauricio ignores Roberto's words, puts on the earphones, and moves the controls.

MAURICIO: *(Coughing. Tired.)* I think the batteries are gone.

ELENA: How long do you think we've got left?

ROBERTO: A whole lifetime. *(He passes his fingers through his hair and notices that it is falling out.)* My hair's falling out already.

Surreptitiously, Mauricio also passes his fingers through his hair and looks at his hand. A long silent pause follows.

ELENA: *(Thinking.)* I wasn't a good daughter, you know? I paid no attention to my parents. I felt they weren't sophisticated, that nothing they said had any relevance. My mother only talked about her illnesses. My father always told the same jokes . . . and got drunk.

ROBERTO: My folks didn't want me to become an actor. They didn't think it was a serious profession. "They're all fags," my father used to tell me. He died of a hernia caused by lifting boxes that were too heavy for him.

MAURICIO: My mother believed everything she saw on TV . . .

The lights blink several times and return dimmer.

ELENA: There're candles in the kitchen.

ROBERTO: I'll get them.

Mauricio sits next to Elena. She embraces him as if he were a child.

ELENA: Don't be scared of the dark, honey. If you think you're surrounded by the same things you could see when the lights were on, you won't be afraid.

MAURICIO: *(Childlike.)* I'm not afraid of the dark, Mommy. But I get bored without the TV. One can't do anything in the dark.

ELENA: Yes, you can. You can play at imagining things, people, places . . . like playing videotapes in your head, you know?

The lights blink again and become ever dimmer. The room is now almost completely dark. Roberto enters with a lighted candle.

MAURICIO: I imagine that . . . that tomorrow the sun will come out like it did before, that I'll go to the beach and . . .

ROBERTO: I imagine that I'm in the boat with Pepe: we're going fishing. It's six o'clock in the morning . . . The sea is calm; the sun isn't hot yet. I row; he talks about baseball . . .

ELENA: I imagine that I am 13. I'm home, in my bedroom, sitting at my tiny desk . . . I write in my diary: "Dear Diary: Today, Friday, March 15, he looked at me and smiled. I thought my heart was going to burst . . . "

MAURICIO: I imagine that . . . nothing has happened . . . that everything's like it was before . . .

ROBERTO: I imagine that I sit down with my son and tell him about the rivers and the deserts, the lakes and the mountains, the shape of the earth; one by one, I point out to him all the wonders of nature . . . *(He coughs.)*

ELENA: I imagine that . . . the smell of fresh crushed garlic fills the entire house. I imagine that my grandma is making my favorite soup. I imagine that . . . I can still remember the smell of fresh crushed garlic . . . *(She coughs and shivers.)*

MAURICIO: I imagine that I'm a television actor: I arrive at the studios and my colleagues are waiting for me . . . the director, the cameramen, the makeup girl. I imagine that we are about to tape the last chapter of . . . "Winter Passion."

Mauricio has a coughing spell. Lights go out completely. Elena lights several candles. She places one on the coffee table. Once the room is lighted by candles, one can see that Elena is wearing a gas mask which gives her an insectlike appearance. She's alone on stage.

ELENA: *(Gazing at the candle. Sighing.)* Candles are so romantic!

Roberto enters, also wearing a gas mask.

ROBERTO: Except when you have to use them out of necessity.

ELENA: Hello, darling! You've come home early today.

ROBERTO: Where's the boy?

Mauricio enters, also wearing a mask.

MAURICIO: Here I am, Dad. I'm feeling lousy . . . *(Coughs.)*

ROBERTO: It must be the flu. Bundle up. *(To Elena.)* Dear, I have a surprise for you. Close your eyes.

ELENA: *(Covering her eyes with her hand over the mask.)* I wonder what it is.

ROBERTO: Open them. Happy anniversary!

Roberto hands Elena a feather duster, pretending it is a bunch of flowers.

ELENA: Such beautiful roses! My favorites! I thought you had forgotten.

ROBERTO: I never forget our anniversary.

They kiss with masks on. The noise of the wind increases.

ELENA: *(Coughing.)* I've prepared a great dinner with all of your favorite dishes.

ROBERTO: *(Coughing.)* You're so wonderful, sweetheart! Let's open that bottle of French wine we've been saving for a special occasion.

Roberto gets the bottle out, opens it, and fills two glasses. They toast each other.

ELENA: You know, dear . . . I'm so happy.

ROBERTO: So am I, my love.

Roberto and Elena freeze, their glasses raised in a toast. Mauricio, sitting on the floor staring at a candle, turns to look at Elena and Roberto, and then looks at the audience. He takes off his mask.

MAURICIO: *(Stepping out of character, coughing, confused, talks to the audience and to himself at the same time.)* But . . . this . . . who's going to understand this?

Elena, back to reality, takes off her mask and speaks out of breath.

ELENA: No one's going to understand it. I don't like this at all.

ROBERTO: *(Takes off his mask, coughing.)* I don't like it either.

MAURICIO: What are we gonna do?

ELENA: What we need are some fresh, new ideas.

ROBERTO: Yes, yes, that's what we need . . .

ELENA: . . . It's getting late . . . Who's got any new ideas?

The three put their gas masks back on and sit very close together on the floor. The candles go out. Only the masks glowing in the dark can be seen.

MAURICIO: *(In the dark. Faintly.)* How about if . . .

Total blackout.

THE END

Notes

[1]Original lyrics: "Algo de mí, algo de mí / se va muriendo. / Quiero vivir, quiero vivir . . . "

[2]Original lyrics: "Y pasaron muchos años de ilusión / entregado a las delicias de mi amor / pero al fin he comprendido / vale más cualquier amigo / sea un borracho, sea un perdido / que la más linda mujer."

[3]Starting with this line, the original Spanish lyrics read:

ELENA: ¿Y tú cómo estás?

MAURICIO: ¿Yo? Encantado de la vida. ¿Y tú cómo estás?

ELENA: Yo, encantada del amor.

MAURICIO: ¿Y cómo fue?

ELENA: No sé explicarme como fue. Fueron sus ojos o su boca. Fueron sus manos o su piel. Fue a lo mejor la impaciencia de tanto esperar . . . [. . .]

ROBERTO: Adiós muchachos, compañeros de mi vida, farras queridas de aquellos tiempos. Me toca a mí hoy emprender la retirada . . .

[4]Starting with this line, the original Spanish lyrics read:

ELENA: Este amor apasionado anda todo alborotado por volver . . .

ROBERTO: Déjame, no quiero que me toques. Por tu culpa estoy sufriendo, la tortura del recuerdo.

MAURICIO: Dame un beso y olvida que me has besado; yo te ofrezco la vida si me la pides . . .

The Marriage of Hippolyta

Manuel Pereiras

Manuel Pereiras

Born in Cifuentes, province of Las Villas, in 1950, Manuel Pereiras came to the United States in 1968. He started writing in 1976 after taking a premeditated overdose of Valium. According to him, the overdose, instead of putting an end to his life, triggered his creativity. His first two plays, *Las hetairas habaneras* (1976) and *The Butterfly Cazador* (1977), a musical, were written in collaboration with José Corrales. His first solo adventures were the theater pieces *America . . .* (1976) and *El mar nuestro de cada día* (1978); both works are dramatic compilations of poetry by Hispanic writers. These works deal with the themes of America (North and South) and suicide, respectively.

In 1980 Pereiras became a founding member of the Stonewall Repertory Theater where his *Holy Night* (*Nochebuena*, 1978), a semifinalist at the Eugene O'Neill Center, was showcased. His *Folk Song* (*Guajira de salón*, 1979) received a staged reading at the Triplex of the Borough of Manhattan Community College in 1984. In 1981 he turned to writing directly in English and wrote *Gabriel* (1981), *All about Muté* (1981), *Still Still* (1983), and *The Marriage of Hippolyta* (1984), his first one-act play which we include here. In December 1985 Pereiras joined María Irene Fornés's workshop at INTAR (International Arts Relations, Inc.). Since then he has completed seven more plays, three of which are full-length.

Manuel Pereiras, who holds graduate degrees in both Spanish Literature and Bilingual Education, has taught for a number of years. In 1985, however, he decided to leave his teaching job to become a full-time playwright. He presently lives in Princeton, New Jersey.

The Marriage of Hippolyta is a thought-provoking drama—loosely based on the myth of the Amazons and the story of Phaedra (Fedora in the play)—which presents a disquieting mother-daughter relationship. A mysterious aura envelopes the dialogue which takes place between Hippolyta, Nardo (her cousin), and Fedora (Hippolyta's mother). Hippolyta realizes her homosexual inclinations during her wedding night, when, out of repulsion, she refuses to consumate her marriage. The experience makes her see the similarity between the man's caresses and her mother's, which she had naively viewed as part of motherly love and not as an expression of incestuous pleasure. As in the case of the mythical Amazons (and there are clear references to them in the text) who removed or flattened their right breast to better use the bow and arrow, Fedora also had her right breast removed—probably, in our present day, because of a malignant growth. Her caressing Hippolyta's breast can be seen at first as a way of admiring in her daughter—a continuation of herself—the breast she has lost, but we finally realize the act was born of a lesbian attraction. The suspense is masterfully maintained until the very end when the truth is revealed and tragedy occurs. Fedora, like Phaedra in the classical myth, commits suicide out of remorse when her passion is unveiled before her daughter's eyes.

The Marriage of Hippolyta

To Georgine Gorra

Characters

NARDO, sixteen. In the first scene she wears an apron because she has just washed her cousin Hippolyta's hair. In the second scene she wears a robe; she has been staying with her aunt, Fedora.

HIPPOLYTA, sixteen. In the first scene she is wrapped in sheets and towels; her hair is wet. For the second scene she wears elegant street clothes of the period.

FEDORA, thirty-three. She wears a slip in both scenes.

Setting

Table and chairs. A door with a curtain.

The action takes place in a room in Fedora's house, during the mid-1950s, in a cold city. One week elapses between the two scenes.

SCENE 1

NARDO: You don't look too happy.
HIPPOLYTA: I'm afraid.
NARDO: Nothing to be afraid of.
HIPPOLYTA: Have you, really?
NARDO: You're about the only one who hasn't.
HIPPOLYTA: I'm afraid.
NARDO: I'm telling you. . .

HIPPOLYTA: It's not only that.
NARDO: What is it?
HIPPOLYTA: Life.
NARDO: Life in general?
HIPPOLYTA: Life with him.
NARDO: It'll be the same as my parents', your parents', everybody!
HIPPOLYTA: That's what I mean.
NARDO: Don't be silly. That's the way it is. Besides, your mother . . .
HIPPOLYTA: She's happy now, isn't she?
NARDO: She seems to be.
HIPPOLYTA: It's good she's found happiness. My father made her miserable.
NARDO: This guy seems to be right for her.
HIPPOLYTA: She loves him. That's why I'm getting married.
NARDO: Don't tell me . . .
HIPPOLYTA: I'm following in their footsteps.
NARDO: If that's the only reason . . .
HIPPOLYTA: I want to know.
NARDO: You really should know by now.
HIPPOLYTA: I don't. Remember that time when we . . . ?
NARDO: You're always reminding me of such childhood nonsense.
HIPPOLYTA: Yes. Such nonsense!
NARDO: When you try the real thing, you'll have no more doubts. I'm so glad you're getting married. And to him! The grapevine has it that . . .
HIPPOLYTA: Please!
NARDO: Come on. All the girls are going to talk about it at the shower.
HIPPOLYTA: In front of Mother?
NARDO: She'll no longer be your mother. She'll be another woman.
HIPPOLYTA: What do you mean?
NARDO: When a woman has a man, all other women are "the other," including your own mother. Especially with a mother like yours.
HIPPOLYTA: You're talking garbage.
NARDO: You'll see.
HIPPOLYTA: My mother never . . .
NARDO: Let me tell you, I wouldn't let my mother come too near any of my boyfriends.
HIPPOLYTA: Nardo!
NARDO: Are we cousins or not?

HIPPOLYTA: You're my dearest.

NARDO: Then why this convent attitude of yours? Mother Eugenia's not listening.

HIPPOLYTA: I need her now.

NARDO: She was a pain.

HIPPOLYTA: She was always so comforting. Besides my mother, she's been the only person whose touch has been really comforting.

NARDO: What about me?

HIPPOLYTA: You don't want to talk about it. Or do you?

NARDO: There's nothing to say.

HIPPOLYTA: I won't say it then. You're also very much like mother.

NARDO: I wish I really were like her.

HIPPOLYTA: In some ways you are and in some you're not.

NARDO: What do you mean?

HIPPOLYTA: You don't like to talk.

NARDO: Your mother never stops talking!

HIPPOLYTA: She's always speaking. I mean talking.

NARDO: And what are we doing?

HIPPOLYTA: Let the time pass and with the time, life, thoughts, love.

NARDO: You'll know love Sunday night.

HIPPOLYTA: Love! I know it . . . and hate too.

NARDO: You're nuts. My mother says one doesn't know what hate is until after ten years of marriage.

HIPPOLYTA: If I didn't know hate, you'd really scare me. But my mother hates me.

NARDO: You're definitely nuts. Your mother adores you.

HIPPOLYTA: Since her operation . . .

NARDO: You have to understand.

HIPPOLYTA: I do, believe me. But one day, in the middle of the night, while I was asleep, she ran into my room and grabbed my breasts and held them tight until it hurt—she really squeezed them—I wanted to scream. But I was afraid and then she started to touch them very softly, rubbing them, tenderly. I felt her breath and she kissed them. All of a sudden she bit one of my nipples so hard that I fainted. I can still feel the pain.

NARDO: You probably dreamed that the night we smoked marijuana.

HIPPOLYTA: It wasn't a dream, though I've dreamed about it since.

NARDO: Was it the right one?

HIPPOLYTA: Yes. She laughs about it. "I'm a real daughter of my country now," she says. "I think that I'm so wild inside because of the jungles."

NARDO: Aunt Fedora has never even seen the jungles. Father always tells me that she was born there by an act of fate.

HIPPOLYTA: Precisely. Fate.

NARDO: Mother Eugenia wouldn't like your relying on fate so much.

HIPPOLYTA: I don't like it either, but I can't help thinking our fate is sealed. When I was a child and heard that phrase I thought that it meant that fate was inside seals. Even though I didn't know what fate was I was afraid of seals, and whenever I went to the zoo, I would avoid the seal pond. Even their sounds made me cry.

NARDO: I love seals.

HIPPOLYTA: Sealed lips.

Fedora enters.

NARDO: They do have ugly lips.

FEDORA: Who has ugly lips?

HIPPOLYTA: Seals, Mother.

FEDORA: But seals are lovely. I've always wanted one as a pet. *(She talks to Hippolyta.)* This is my seal. And her lips are very nice. *(She kisses Hippolyta on the mouth.)* Did I hurt you?

HIPPOLYTA: A little. My lips are dry.

FEDORA: They've always been dry. You are dry. A woman's lips should be soft. Touch mine. *(Takes Hippolyta's hands to bring them to her lips.)*

HIPPOLYTA: *(As she rejects the action.)* I know they're soft, Mother.

FEDORA: You don't even want to touch me anymore. You've become a woman. A regular fickle woman with the idea that every other woman's your rival. You've probably been listening to your cousin here and the flimsy ideas her mother puts in her head. But the only one a woman can ever trust is another woman. Aren't you sleeping well? Look at those circles around her eyes, Nardo. You have to tell her how sweet a man can be when he's eager. I've heard you know a lot . . .

HIPPOLYTA: Mother, please.

NARDO: Let her be. It's all right. I understand. With her problems and all . . .

HIPPOLYTA: Nardo!

FEDORA: My problem? Oh, yes! My problem! My problem is that I still have feelings in the tit I don't have. Imagine how much feeling I have in what I have left. *(Addresses Nardo.)* Do you have any feelings?

HIPPOLYTA: Mother!

FEDORA: Am I your mother? Answer me! Am I your mother? Your real mother? Answer!

HIPPOLYTA: Yes!

FEDORA: How do you know! I wouldn't know you're my daughter by looking at you. Look at your hair.

NARDO: Her hair's lovely.

FEDORA: Let me braid it.

HIPPOLYTA: It's still wet, Mother.

FEDORA: Wet. I'm wet, too. And my husband's not here to dry this wetness. Give me that comb. *(Nardo does. Fedora braids Hippolyta's hair.)* You're looking very nice, Nardo. Did the dress fit you? I used to be as skinny as you at your age but I was always broad in the hips. *(Hippolyta tries to raise her head to participate in the conversation, but Fedora keeps pushing it down. She talks to Hippolyta.)* Keep your head down. *(Talks to Nardo.)* Are you getting married soon, Nardo?

NARDO: If I want to.

FEDORA: And with whom you want? I doubt it. Men don't like antiques. You're young, but you've been around . . . How did that joke about the furniture go? Never mind. Hippolyta used to have blonde curly hair. When I threw her father out, her hair turned straight and dark. She's hated me since. And I've hated her hair. Do you feel my hate, Hippolyta? It's creeping off my fingers. I hope when you grow older, women can keep their hair long. When I was a kid, women were allowed to keep their hair long, but as they grew older they had to wear it in a bun. Now we have to cut it once we pass thirty or we're taken for prostitutes. I hope there'll be a time when women can wear their hair as they want.

HIPPOLYTA: *(Raising her head.)* I want mine short, Mother.

FEDORA: *(As she pushes her head down.)* I mean women, not kids.

NARDO: We're not kids.

FEDORA: Bah! When we were your age, we were adults. Your mother and I married when we were even younger than Hippolyta. But we were ready. Kids nowadays know a lot of things we didn't know back then, but I think all that knowledge keeps them from growing, from maturing. When I was Hippolyta's age . . . How does the dress fit?

NARDO: All right.

FEDORA: You don't like it? It was your mother's idea. I was her maid of honor; you'll be Hippolyta's. She's wearing her dress; you're wearing mine. *(Finishes braid.)* Let me look at you. *(Hippolyta sits up.)* You really look like a horse.

NARDO: Why do you let your mother . . . ?

HIPPOLYTA: She loves horses.

FEDORA: They're wonderful: so beautiful, so strong, so proud. But in the end, men tame them. Will you ever be tamed, Hippolyta, my wild horse? You're no fluke. I wanted you to be all I wasn't, and you're making all the same mistakes. I hope you don't make them twice as I've done.

HIPPOLYTA: But you're happy, Mother.

FEDORA: He's all right. At least, he's not a drunkard. But men, like their erections, are so obvious. Some women are obvious too: look at your cousin here. Pretty as a doll. And as dull. I wish I were a doll. I'm a mere tamed mare. What time's the shower? Is anybody coming? You have so few friends, darling. I know it's my fault—I shouldn't call it a fault. Most people are parasites. They live off you; they suck your feelings, your thoughts and give nothing in return. Friendships should be symbiotic relationships. I wanted to be a biologist, Nardo.

NARDO: And go into the jungle.

FEDORA: Sure, laugh. And go into the jungle where I belong.

NARDO: You weren't born . . .

FEDORA: Does it matter? I'm an Amazon, aren't I, Hippolyta?

HIPPOLYTA: *(Childlike. Plays a game she and her mother have played many times before, a game very real to her.)* Yes, Mother. Oh, yes, you are, Mother. And one day I'll take you on my back back to the jungle.

NARDO: The Amazons aren't from Brazil. In our mythology class . . .

HIPPOLYTA: We're not talking myths: we're talking reality.

NARDO: *(Jealous of the other two's closeness.)* Like that dream about your mother?

FEDORA: What dream was that?

NARDO: *(After Hippolyta's silent reproach, to her.)* I'm sorry.

HIPPOLYTA: Nothing, Mother.

FEDORA: Nothing. I know. That's all you've ever given me. That's all anybody's ever given me. I don't care about anybody. I care about you. And when are you taking me back to the jungle? After your husband has destroyed you?

HIPPOLYTA: You married first, Mother.

FEDORA: Nardo came first.

NARDO: What do I have to do . . . ?

FEDORA: What indeed? The shower. You have to attend to the shower. Why are we having it so late? What took you so long to set a date, Nardo?

HIPPOLYTA: I wasn't sure, Mother.

FEDORA: You weren't sure! And you were letting me spend all that money? I'm not rich, you know?

HIPPOLYTA: I know. That's why I changed my mind.

FEDORA: I'm not that poor.

HIPPOLYTA: It's better this way.

FEDORA: At least you're proud. Friday's a good day for a shower. Frigga's the goddess of marriages. She might shower you with happiness. The Latins dedicated this date to Venus. But we have always been duller; we passed up Freya and gave it to Frigga. Did you know that Frigga means both woman and wife? We've been blasted since ancient times. We've been made to believe that we're no woman if we're no wife. Woman also means a man's wife. Man means human being. I think what woman really means is a human being with woes. Sorrows. I wished they had named me Dolores. Maybe if I had been born in a Spanish-speaking country . . . My mother wanted to name me Theodora, God's gift, after so many boys finally . . . But my father said he was sure that they'd conceived me in a quickie, that mother hadn't even had time to take off her hat and so I was named after a hat. Some people show no respect for their offspring. Your name's rather strange too, Nardo.

NARDO: I don't care. I'd be the same no matter what.

FEDORA: Nardo by any other name . . . Flowers! Flowers for the dead. Wreathes. Wreathes for the dead. *(Talks to Hippolyta.)* La iglesia llena de flores: tu tumba. *(Holds Hippolyta's head, tight.)* The Spanish people have a saying: "Husbands and death are sent by Heaven." Isn't it redundant? *(Squeezes Hippolyta's head.)* I've made sure the church will be flooded with flowers on Sunday.

HIPPOLYTA: You're hurting me, Mother.
NARDO: Stop it!
FEDORA: *(Without letting go.)* Flowers, flowers for the bride.

SCENE 2

NARDO: She's coming today, isn't she?
FEDORA: So she said.
NARDO: Was she happy?
FEDORA: How should I know?
NARDO: Does she sound like it?
FEDORA: What does happiness sound like?
NARDO: You should know. Father says you were a happy child.
FEDORA: I was a clown.
NARDO: I love the circus.
FEDORA: Yes, they're all right. I should like the circus too; it would go with my personality, but I don't.
NARDO: Yes, they're free.
FEDORA: I don't know about that. Everything must be perfect or it becomes a fiasco. Then perfection's the real fiasco. We're constantly falling off trapezes and getting back on. Or are we constant spectators? You bring the worst out in me. You make me talk strange. My thoughts aren't like this at all.
NARDO: I don't know how my thoughts are.
FEDORA: Do you have any?
NARDO: Let's wait for Hippolyta in a nice mood.
FEDORA: We owe it to her, don't we? . . . that is, if we owe anybody anything. There I go again.
NARDO: What are you thinking about?
FEDORA: I don't know exactly. What should I think about?
NARDO: Hippolyta.
FEDORA: *(Putting on a blank face. Pause.)* That's how.
NARDO: How?
FEDORA: If I tell you . . . *(A door is heard.)*
NARDO: Is that her?
FEDORA: Hippolyta? Hippolyta, is that you?
HIPPOLYTA: *(Enters.)* I think so.
FEDORA: You look . . .
NARDO: Beautiful . . .

FEDORA: Radiant . . .
HIPPOLYTA: I know myself now.
NARDO: What did I tell you!
FEDORA: You do, don't you?
HIPPOLYTA: I do.
NARDO: Tell us.
HIPPOLYTA: You have to experience it, Nardo.
NARDO: I have, you know.
FEDORA: She's not talking about that.
NARDO: She's not?
FEDORA: I don't think so.
HIPPOLYTA: Are you always right, Mother?
FEDORA: I talk a lot of nonsense.
HIPPOLYTA: That too.
NARDO: Is he really . . . ?
FEDORA: Always after that.
NARDO: Aren't we all?
HIPPOLYTA: Are we, dear Nardo? Come, sit on my lap. Let me show you what he did to me. *(Nardo goes to Hippolyta ready for the game. Fedora shows her displeasure.)*
NARDO: *(Sits on Hippolyta's lap.)* Should I sit like this?
HIPPOLYTA: It doesn't matter. He'd reach you. If you know what I mean.
NARDO: Hey! I feel it.
HIPPOLYTA: *(She will act out what she is describing from now on.)* He held me tight by my waist with one arm and put his other hand up my skirt, like this.
FEDORA: *(Does not like what is going on at all.)* Stop it!
HIPPOLYTA: I am a woman now, Mother.
NARDO: Ah, that's hot!
HIPPOLYTA: And he got closer and closer. And he started playing with it.
NARDO: *(Realizes it is more than a game.)* Hippolyta!
HIPPOLYTA: *(Like a lion tamer.)* Quiet.
FEDORA: *(Forceful.)* Stop it!
NARDO: *(Afraid.)* Let me go.
HIPPOLYTA: Quiet. And he kept on playing. Like this, Nardo. Isn't it exciting?
NARDO: *(Completely afraid, pulling away.)* Let me go.

HIPPOLYTA: *(Keeping her on her lap.)* Isn't it exciting, Nardo? My hand's not as strong as his and you cannot feel me from behind and my finger's not as thick as his but you get the idea, don't you?

FEDORA: *(Reproachful.)* Hippolyta.

HIPPOLYTA: And do you want to know what I did? *(To Fedora.)* You come and sit too, Mother. Don't you leave us, Nardo. *(Nardo is in shock.)* You should watch this part now as Mother watched yours. Sit, Mother. I'll play myself.

FEDORA: Children's play.

HIPPOLYTA: I'm a woman, Mother. I know I'm a woman, Mother. Sit. *(Fedora takes up the challenge, daringly. She sits on Hippolyta's lap.)* That's it. Where were we? He's been caressing my . . . thighs. Yes, Mother, just like that. *(Fedora also acts out what Hippolyta describes.)* And he has brought his hand to where we feel and he puts his other hand on my breast, Mother. Leave it there, Mother, and play with it. And all this time I was thinking how different it had been with you, Nardo. How different were our little, innocent games. And how different from Mother's washing and rubbing of baby powder. How can I remember? Her soft hand in my crotch. *(Fedora is fully into it.)* And it was so different I got wild, really wild, like now. Don't you see how wild I am? I turned to him and kissed him. Do you want to see, Nardo?

NARDO: No!

HIPPOLYTA: Are you sure, Nardo?

NARDO: I'm leaving.

HIPPOLYTA: *(The lion tamer in total command.)* You're staying, Nardo. Play your part. Mother's playing hers to the hilt. Better than I expected. I turned to him and kissed him. Like this.

NARDO: No!

Hippolyta and Fedora kiss passionately for a while.

NARDO: No!

HIPPOLYTA: No. I didn't kiss him. I was nauseated, disgusted by his touching. I got up. I spit on his face and slapped him. *(Acts this out too.)* Just like Mother, he didn't react. And I apologized. It hadn't been his intention, but he has been the only one who's told me the truth. The truth that, the world, you, and Mother, especially Mother, have been hiding.

FEDORA: *(Defeated.)* I've always tried to . . .

HIPPOLYTA: You tried to conceal everything.

FEDORA: I've always hinted.

HIPPOLYTA: Hints aren't answers, Mother.

FEDORA: A word to the wise . . .

HIPPOLYTA: Were you testing me, Mother?

FEDORA: *(Defiant.)* Yes. I was testing you. Don't you come to me and tell me I did wrong. How much clearer did you want it?

HIPPOLYTA: I wanted it transparent.

FEDORA: It was. As transparent as things are allowed to be. *(Giving up again.)* But it was covered with a black curtain. And that's the way you should have let it . . . Or . . .

HIPPOLYTA: *(Hopeful.)* Or what?

FEDORA: It's too late.

HIPPOLYTA: It's not. I can take you to the jungle. *(Grabs Fedora, ready to flee.)* I'm not destroyed.

FEDORA: I am. Let me go. I must rest. *(Hippolyta lets her go. Fedora leaves, destroyed but proud.)*

NARDO: *(Not believing what has happened.)* What have you gained?

HIPPOLYTA: I don't know yet. What about you?

NARDO: I know I've lost nothing. I'm not what you think.

HIPPOLYTA: Don't blind yourself.

NARDO: No; you can blame me because I knew. I'm generally dumb but not about these things. And believe me, we are different.

HIPPOLYTA: All women are one: me, you, Mother . . . *(A horrible scream is heard.)* Mother? *(She yells.)* Mother! *(Hippolyta exits. Pause. Then she enters, incredulous, defiant, proud.)*

NARDO: What is it?

HIPPOLYTA: *(Matter-of-factly.)* She's stabbed herself.

NARDO: It isn't possible. Let's call . . .

HIPPOLYTA: Don't. The wound's too big. She ripped open her womb.

NARDO: Oh, no.

HIPPOLYTA: Her guts are all over the floor.

NARDO: Stop.

HIPPOLYTA: The blood's all over the room.

NARDO: *(In total shock, but angry.)* How . . . can . . . you . . . be . . . so . . . calm?

HIPPOLYTA: We must stop one day doing to ourselves what they do to us. This is as good a time to start as any other. Why don't you start too, Nardo? *(To the audience.)* And how about you?

Perhaps the Marshland

Héctor Pérez

Héctor Pérez

Héctor Pérez was born in Havana in 1957. At the age of five he left his native Cuba with his parents. Educated in the United States, he earned an Associate of Arts degree (1980) in theater from Miami-Dade Community College and a Bachelor of Arts degree (1982) also in theater from Florida State University in Tallahassee. In 1982 the Fine Arts Council of Florida in conjunction with the National Endowment for the Arts awarded him an Individual Artist Fellowship in Playwriting.

Pérez, who writes in English, is the author of three major plays to date: *Tabletop* (1981), *Perhaps the Marshland* (1982), and *Stalactites* (1986). The first two were produced by Etc. Theater of Tallahassee, Florida, in 1983. There was also a reading of *Perhaps the Marshland* by the theatrical group New Theater of Miami in 1986. At present, Pérez is an independent writer and producer of public information materials for various human services agencies in Tampa, Florida, where he lives.

Perhaps the Marshland—with its allusion to resettlement and genocide—points to the predicament of certain human groups whenever racial, religious, or political prejudices prevail in a society. The peasants, the army, the secret police, the special guard, threats often mentioned in the play, become a living presence on stage through the powerful metaphor of the darkness that is falling upon the characters. It is in this context that the clearing in the forest where the action takes place acquires its full significance as the last "known" territory in which the pursued may seek refuge from the unnamed pursuers. Beyond lies the marshland, the "unknown," with its promise of a possible new beginning and the threat of an uncertain death. The author also suggests a reason for hope in Bumboy, the orphan, who, under the care and guidance of Franz, the outcast, may live to bring about a new start.

Perhaps the Marshland

Characters

BUMBOY, an eight-year-old boy.
BLOCH, a forty-seven-year-old man with a voracious appetite.
FRANZ, a slender, thirty-five-year-old man who seems fifty.
ARK, a sixty-year-old man with a high, prominent forehead.
SERBIUS, an eighteen-year-old youth on the verge of manhood. Ark's son.

Setting

The action takes place at twilight, during the present.

A bleak clearing in the forest. The branches hang from the trees like twisted marionettes. Beyond this clearing lie the marshlands. The trees and bushes appear like the jagged edges of a shattered window. There is a pitifully small campfire in the clearing.

As the lights go on, smoke slowly rises from the ashes of the campfire. Bumboy is picking attentively at Bloch's shirt. Bloch, in long underwear, paces back and forth. Ark and Serbius are finishing their soup. With extreme care, Franz sips his.

BLOCH: Louse! Damn you, boy . . . I gave you my shirt an hour ago.
BUMBOY: *(Shaking.)* Plea . . .
BLOCH: Stop being such a spastic and delouse that stinking shirt. I'll whip you if you don't hurry up.
FRANZ: Those bugs are hard to get to.
ARK You should leave the boy alone.
BLOCH: Why? He's mine.
SERBIUS: Mister, he's only a child.

FRANZ: They're wingless.

BLOCH: What's that?

FRANZ: *(Very positively.)* They can't fly. I'm sure that if you look deeply, you'll find columns of them. Put the shirt on the ground and stomp on it.

Bumboy puts the shirt on the ground and is about to stomp on it.

SERBIUS: Make sure you get the ringleader.

BUMBOY: Yeah.

BLOCH: Bumboy, I'll kick you if you put a foot on that shirt. You're mine. Therefore, what I say goes.

Bumboy stops and slinks back to his corner with the shirt.

BLOCH: Good.

SERBIUS: You've been barking for the last two days, and our situation hasn't improved.

ARK: Be quiet.

SERBIUS: Look at him. He's a rat. You'd be better off if you ran into the forest, Bloch.

FRANZ: Or perhaps the marshland.

BLOCH: You said you were going to get us bread.

SERBIUS: If we wait here, the invading forces from the East will trample us. And if I go into the village, the peasants will attack me with their superstitious tongues and axes. Actually, I'm more afraid of their vicious tongues than the axes.

ARK: That's always the most lethal.

BLOCH: Don't be so hard on us peasants.

SERBIUS: The boy ought to delouse your beard.

ARK: Will you sleep tonight, Bloch?

BLOCH: Leave me alone. I'll sleep when I want to. The Bumboy watches over me. He never rests at night. You might slit my throat in the dark and steal the boy.

Franz, who has been sipping his soup from a rusty can, looks up at Bloch.

ARK: We want you to set the boy free. He's nothing to you. He's not your blood. *(Pause.)* There'll be no more abusing the boy.

BLOCH: I'll amuse myself as I wish. *(To Ark.)* And no dog of a city official can tell me what to do. We're all exiles in this forest. *(Pause.)* Ark, what about the bread?

FRANZ: With this can.

SERBIUS: What are you saying, Franz?

FRANZ: Cut Bloch's jugular vein with this rusty can while he snores.

BLOCH: *(Upset.)* You grave robber. Why did we feed him? Look at his clothes—all different. He's a mongrel and a ghoul. You're an escapee, aren't you?

FRANZ: *(Ignoring Bloch's question.)* Why do you call him Bumboy?

BLOCH: Can't you see anything with your infected eyes? He's a waif. It was me who saved the poor boy. It was me that came across his mangled body in the birch bushes alongside the railroad tracks. That was two years ago. He must have been in a transport. His family probably threw him out of the window to save him.

Franz flings his cup at Bloch.

BLOCH: You filthy scum. They should've killed you. You know about the freight cars . . . where they go. I'm just an ignorant farmer.

SERBIUS: And you stink.

FRANZ: *(He points to Bumboy.)* He's why the war's being fought. I know that much.

SERBIUS: It'd be wiser if you disappeared into the forest, Bloch, minus the boy.

BLOCH: No. He took care of my goats and fed grass to my rabbits. I gave the enemy my crops, my house . . . I was at the market with the boy selling turnips and milk . . . when I got back, there was nothing. *(Pause.)* I saved the boy. The Bumboy's all I have.

FRANZ: Are you sure he came from a transport?

BLOCH: Are you calling me a liar?

FRANZ: *(Shaking his head.)* He's a gift.

BLOCH: My family called him a pest. My village friends, that I hated, called him a pixie. If I hadn't taken care of the little guy, he'd have died on his own. Right, Bumboy?

BUMBOY: Yeah.

BLOCH: He has cat's eyes. He can scare you with just a glance.

SERBIUS: Bloch, you clown. You're worse than the peasants that have chased us into this forest.

ARK: The bread, Serbius.

SERBIUS: I'm going.

BLOCH: If you find some sausage, bring it back.

SERBIUS: Sausage? Are you kidding?

ARK: My boy's risking enough.

BLOCH: Look for rabbits. Their meat would be good.

Through all this conversation, Franz has been concentrating on Bumboy.

FRANZ: You're right, Bloch.

BLOCH: *(Surprised.)* Ha. Finally you say something nice to me. After a day and a half, the spook has a kind word. *(To the others.)* What about that? *(Bumboy is impressed.)* Serbius, just snap the hare's neck.

FRANZ: The Bumboy's eyes are like a whirlpool.

ARK: So are yours.

FRANZ: Yes, but they're not young, and a thin layer of membrane covers them. There's not much of a reflection left in mine.

ARK: Don't get upset. We'll have food tonight, and tomorrow with a full belly . . .

BLOCH: We should stay here.

ARK: It's not wise. Sooner than you think the army or the peasants will find us. Serbius can't continue to raid the farms at night. They might find him.

SERBIUS: Father, we have to live.

ARK: It's dark out there. *(Pause.)* Hurry, you must be in and out quickly, or you won't be able to find your way back.

BLOCH: I can start a small fire.

FRANZ: No.

ARK: No.

BLOCH: Who'd come out here looking for us?

ARK: The special guard.

FRANZ: Maybe you can go tonight, Bloch?

BLOCH: Me? Fat and clumsy as an ox. Serbius is young and spry.

Ark brings Serbius closer to him so they can talk.

ARK: *(Pause.)* No chances now. *(Serbius nods affirmatively.)* If the wind stirs, you turn and scurry back.

Bumboy begins to chuckle.

SERBIUS: Father, I'm not a squirrel.

BLOCH: Bumboy.

Bumboy stops laughing.

ARK: We can manage for a few days without food.

SERBIUS: But we can't move. Where are we going to get our strength from . . . by eating plant roots? The marshlands are about six kilometers away. How can we survive the trek through them? *(Pause.)* The forest has ended, Father. Can't you see? There's no place to hide.

ARK: We can wait.

SERBIUS: For how long?

ARK: A day.

SERBIUS: It's too late. The secret police control even the length of the day. *(Serbius pulls on his coat and readies himself by scrubbing some dirt on his face.) (Calmly.)* I'll be careful. I refuse to be a crumpled piece of paper in someone's hip pocket.

Ark hugs Serbius.

FRANZ: The paper's already in the waste disposal, Serbius. We're nothing but the gray and black streaks of a lead pencil. *(Pause.)* Ark's giving you good advice.

SERBIUS: I promise to return before it's completely dark.

BLOCH: Serbius!

SERBIUS: When I get back, Bloch, I'll barter food for the boy. If you refuse, then you'll starve.

BLOCH: *(Quietly.)* Serbius, you don't have the heart to watch me starve.

ARK: It's agreed. If you don't exchange Bumboy for the food Serbius brings back, then you'll have to fetch your own share.

BLOCH: I can run into the forest.

FRANZ: Without the boy.

SERBIUS: Awkward and misshapen, Bloch? What luck would you have? Nothing awaits you but the farmer's sickle.

Serbius begins to leave as Bloch calls to him.

BLOCH: Serbius! Liverwurst.

Serbius leaves through the forest. Bloch turns to where Bumboy sits.

Ark is overcome by the departure and stands motionless as Franz quietly stares into space.

FRANZ: He did the right thing. He's a courageous young man.

ARK: It gets dark so fast these days. I think it has something to do with winter. It's very hard to keep track of the seasons anymore. There was a time when you knew what to expect. The worst storm could be raging outside but you knew that it would ease. It had to. Those were the laws of nature, and if not of nature, then of man.

BLOCH: *(Listening.)* Man's a beast, Ark, just like nature. It can storm for only so long.

ARK: How far do you think the next farmhouse is, Bloch?

BLOCH: Four thousand meters.

ARK: That far?

BLOCH: I'm sure more.

ARK: No! That's preposterous.

BLOCH: You're calling me a liar?

ARK: Four thousand meters? That's the most absurd thing I've heard. We don't even know where we are. In all honesty, how can you make such a statement?

FRANZ: *(Interjecting.)* There was no record of it.

ARK: *(Confused.)* Of the figures? *(Pause.)* Bloch doesn't know what he's talking about.

BLOCH: *(Irritated.)* Don't call me an idiot.

ARK: It suits you.

FRANZ: It's not his fault, Ark.

ARK: I won't have you defending him. You see, he calls himself an idiot before the word is even out of my mouth. That defines him.

Bloch crouches as if to attack Ark.

BLOCH: I'll twist your arm until it breaks.

Franz makes a move to come between Bloch and Ark.

FRANZ: All I said was that we've never been in this part of the forest. Even the imagination can't chart the depths of it. Four thousand meters, perhaps five. There's no record of the farmhouse or the distance to the forest.

BLOCH: *(Satisfied.)* You see. Good.

ARK: *(To Bloch.)* My son has the bread. The crumbs of your life are in his hands. You can't scare this old man with bullying threats.

Bumboy pulls at Bloch's shirt and whispers in his ear.

FRANZ: What does Bumboy want?
BLOCH: Liverwurst.

Ark turns and goes to sit by himself.

FRANZ: Is he cold? The night's coming on with a freezing chill.
BLOCH: Ask him. I'm not an interpreter.
FRANZ: *(Sincerely.)* Are you cold, Bumboy?

Bumboy looks to Bloch who does not want to be bothered. Confused by the show of concern, Bumboy turns to Franz who has not taken his eyes off him.

BUMBOY: *(Apologetic.)* Yeah.
FRANZ: *(To Bloch.)* How can he talk to you?

Bloch motions Bumboy to come stand near him.

BLOCH: With his lips and tongue, how else? Show the mongrel your tongue, Bumboy. *(Bumboy sticks out his tongue.)* You see, a perfect specimen. *(Bumboy's tongue is still hanging out.)* Pull it back in, Bumboy. *(Bumboy does so.)* He talks to me, and me alone. I've trained him not to speak to strangers.
FRANZ: Would you like to get warmer, Bumboy?

Bumboy looks at Bloch who approves.

BUMBOY: Fire. *(He points to the camp fire.)*

Ark turns around immediately.

FRANZ: We can't. Someone's bound to spot it.
ARK: It might be a worthwhile idea, Franz. That way Serbius can find us on his way back.
FRANZ: No.

Ark, dejected, turns around again.

FRANZ: Do you want a shirt, Bumboy?
BUMBOY: Yeah.

Franz takes off his heavy shirt only to reveal that he has another underneath. Franz is wearing several layers of shirts and pants, all mismatched.

FRANZ: *(Handing Bumboy the shirt.)* You must appreciate this shirt, Bumboy. Put it on slowly.

Bloch is enjoying the event very much. Ark is preoccupied with Serbius's absence. Bumboy puts on the shirt slowly.

FRANZ: You're doing very well, Bumboy. Bloch doesn't give you enough credit. *(Bloch laughs.)* Putting on the appropriate garment is always of the utmost importance. *(Bumboy now has the shirt on.)* Bravo. You look splendid.

Bumboy is very proud of himself.

BLOCH: *(Amused.)* Roll the sleeves up.

ARK: *(To Franz.)* Your game's not in good taste. My son hasn't come back and you play charades with the ox. Just look at the night. It has gotten dark so quickly.

FRANZ: Nature's gone haywire.

ARK: And Serbius?

BLOCH: He'll retrace his footsteps.

ARK: In the dark? *(Ark moves away from them but nonetheless continues to listen.)*

BLOCH: He won't forget the bread.

FRANZ: Bumboy, are your legs cold?

BUMBOY: *(Delighted.)* Yeah, yeah.

FRANZ: What you need are socks. Long wool socks to keep your legs warm.

BUMBOY: Socks!

BLOCH: *(Upset.)* Don't clothe him completely or he'll come to expect more.

FRANZ: *(Pleased.)* A decent idea, Bloch.

BLOCH: I treat the boy accordingly, right, Bumboy?

Bumboy nods his head.

FRANZ: Well then, one sock. *(Franz quickly takes off one shoe and rolls down the sock and holds it in the air. He still has two other socks on.)* You see. *(Franz waves the sock.)* One sock per ankle. I do hope that's equitable, Bloch?

BLOCH: That's a fair gesture, vampire.

FRANZ: Here, Bumboy, put your foot into this sock.

Bumboy tries to put the oversized sock on his leg. He does this by hopping on the other foot. When he finally succeeds the sock comes up to his knee. Bloch is laughing at Bumboy.

ARK: He's my last child. *(Pause.)* How can he find his way back, Franz?

FRANZ: *(Not paying attention.)* Ark?

ARK: The farmer's dogs will sniff him in the air.

BLOCH: *(Pats Bumboy on the head.)* Good, Bumboy. Good.

FRANZ: He still has time.

ARK: *(Distant.)* You're being silly and frivolous. Don't make Bumboy into a dancing bear. *(Pause.)* I wish I had a single match, Franz. I'd begin by burning one single leaf. It wouldn't take more than that to turn this forest ablaze.

FRANZ: *(Concerned.)* Maybe he thought it'd be safer to hide in the bushes until dawn.

BLOCH: If he doesn't bring back the sausage, Bumboy stays with me.

ARK: The forest is so inhumanly dark, Franz. If you take as few as eight steps and make any kind of turn, you're lost. Eight steps, guaranteed.

BLOCH: The vampire's right, Ark. Serbius will return with my bread. *(Pause.)* Any more tricks?

FRANZ: It's late. *(Pause.)* The boy'll keep guard while you sleep, Bloch.

BLOCH: For me alone.

FRANZ: Was the boy crying when you found him?

BLOCH: No, he wasn't. What a strange question, jerk. *(He points to Ark.)* Don't lose your mind like him.

FRANZ: A railroad car, Bumboy?

BUMBOY: Yeah.

FRANZ: Do you like your new clothes?

BUMBOY: *(Smiling.)* Yeah.

FRANZ: You've got a fine sentinel, Bloch. *(Pause.)* But his other calf's exposed.

BLOCH: So?

FRANZ: He needs a pant leg.

BLOCH: Ha, ha, ha!

FRANZ: Look at him. His left leg will fall asleep during the night because of the cold.

BLOCH: He has a blanket.

FRANZ: A blanket isn't a pant leg. A sentry slow to react can cost you your life.

BLOCH: Bumboy, your stupid leg is a danger to me. *(Bloch is about to slap Bumboy.)* Are you trying to have me killed?

FRANZ: Bloch!

BUMBOY: No! *(Bumboy circles away from Bloch and moves closer to Ark.)*

ARK: He's the only boy left. Don't hit him.

BLOCH: I'll do with him what I want.

Franz, wearing several layers of clothing, hurriedly takes off his pants and shows them to Bloch.

FRANZ: He can wear this. A pant leg for his honor. This definitely assures you, Bloch, of a sound night's sleep.

BLOCH: Bumboy!

Bumboy quickly puts on the pants that are too big for him. He rolls the pant legs to his ankles. A pair of suspenders holds up the rest. Bumboy looks rather proud in his new clothes.

FRANZ: A faithful and well-dressed guardian. *(Bumboy smiles.)* I salute you, Bumboy. Sweet dreams with your lice, Bloch.

BLOCH: You're a thief and a vampire . . . so many clothes.

ARK: Night has fallen.

BLOCH: Bumboy, an eye on each of them.

BUMBOY: Yeah.

ARK: The night creaks like the rusted hinges of a casket. And there's nothing to prop it open.

FRANZ: You don't dress like a beggar anymore, Bumboy.

BLOCH: *(He moves to the ground to sleep, covering himself tightly with a blanket.)* Bumboy, give me your blanket. *(Bumboy does so.)*

ARK: *(Suddenly.)* Franz?

FRANZ: Go to sleep.

ARK: No. Did you hear the wind?

FRANZ: No. There's no wind tonight.

ARK: Precisely, Franz. Then what was the noise that I just heard?

FRANZ: What noise?

ARK: *(Pointing to the forest.)* It came from there.

FRANZ: Bumboy, did you hear a noise?

BUMBOY: No.

ARK: *(Pause.)* Maybe it's Serbius.

BLOCH: *(Sitting up.)* Serbius? Where? Did he bring me the liverwurst?

BUMBOY: *(Daringly.)* And the bread?

FRANZ: It's no one. Those were probably animals stirring.

BLOCH *and* BUMBOY, *together.* BLOCH: A wild bird. BUMBOY: A squirrel.

ARK: Yes, a squirrel. Serbius is trying to find his way back. Franz, it's damned dark in there. I should go out and walk around. *(Pause.)* I can whistle to him.

FRANZ: Stay here. You'll only get yourself lost.

ARK: Not even a few feet?

FRANZ: You'll trip and bang into the trees. You'll be confused within minutes after your first steps in the dark. Serbius can handle himself.

ARK: He promised to be back by nightfall.

BLOCH: It doesn't matter.

ARK: *(Angry.)* What are you saying, Bloch?

BLOCH: Just that I won't have to cheat you.

ARK: He's my last child.

FRANZ: You were going to give Bumboy to Serbius.

BLOCH: I was hungry.

ARK: You have to let the boy go, Bloch.

BLOCH: I meant to give you Bumboy for one night only. I just needed for my belly to be full. The Bumboy would never go with you, right, Bumboy?

BUMBOY: *(Dejectedly.)* Yeah.

BLOCH: You don't understand. He's mine the way my goats were mine. He would only have run away from you and come back to me.

FRANZ: Not if he knew who he was.

BLOCH: He's an orphan who belongs to Bloch. *(He laughs heartedly while Bumboy seems sad.)*

ARK: He's the last hope in this wilderness. And you have no right to him. As you said . . . he was thrown from a transport.

BLOCH: I took the risk of being found out. You can't hide foreign people.

FRANZ: You used him as labor.

BLOCH: He would have died in those bushes. The railroad guards would have seen him the next day.

FRANZ: He'll come to hate you for that.

BLOCH: *(Skeptical.)* Him? He looks ridiculous in those clothes. Who did you have to assault to get the clothes, grave robber?

FRANZ: *(Disturbed.)* No one.

BLOCH: You've made the Bumboy look like a mutt.

ARK: You're the dog, Bloch.

BLOCH: Curb your tongue, old man. Serbius isn't here anymore, and you can't intimidate me with the threat of no food . . . so . . . watch out.

ARK: You wouldn't have enjoyed the sausage. Your taste, like your conscience, is nil.

FRANZ: Go to sleep, Ark.

ARK: Maybe he's lying in the fields afraid to move . . . his face close to the ground. *(Pause.)* That's it! I'll put my ear to the ground. If he comes, I can listen. *(Ark puts his ear to the ground.)* Franz, I can't hear anything. The earth's dead.

Bumboy, mimicking Ark, puts his ear to the ground. When he arises, Bumboy's face is stricken as if the earth did die.

BLOCH: *(Agitated.)* Bumboy, get up.

BUMBOY: *(He begins to sob.)* It's dead.

ARK: *(Pondering.)* Just to go into the marshlands.

BLOCH: Stop it, Bumboy.

Bloch is about to strike Bumboy, but when Bumboy sees this, he coils up into a ball so that you can't see even his head.

BLOCH: *(Pointing to Ark.)* He's a lunatic.

FRANZ: One might survive in the marshlands. The soldiers won't go in there after us. Serbius was right. The forest has ended.

ARK: The journey's too long for an old man.

BLOCH: Especially for one with bad ears.

FRANZ: You won't attempt the marshland, will you, Bloch?

BLOCH: The war'll be over soon.

FRANZ: You can eat wild mushrooms and oats, Bumboy.

BLOCH: And live like a savage. I have the Bumboy to fetch me food.

FRANZ: The special guard will smell you out, Bloch.

BLOCH: I'm a farmer with nothing except this dumb boy. People will pity my terrible lot. They won't harm us when they find us. I can offer them my neck. Enough of this. *(Pause.)* An eye on each of them. *(Bloch settles down to sleep. He's very tired and will place himself a distance from Bumboy and the rest.)* You've been good, Bumboy.

FRANZ: *(Quietly.)* Yes, you have.

ARK: You should rest, Franz.

FRANZ: If only I could.

ARK: I'll remain waiting for Serbius. If I have nothing else to do, I'll die in this abysmal clearing.

FRANZ: He's young.

ARK: You'd do better to lie down.

FRANZ: Only to be smothered by these clothes. *(Pause.)* You do well to watch out for your son. I'm an anonymous tailor's mannequin, Ark.

ARK: *(Worried.)* Your eyes are like butterfly nets. *(Ark slowly crosses to a corner and crouches, anticipating Serbius's return. He looks forgotten. He will remain listening to what is being said.)*

FRANZ: They've been torn. *(Pause.)* Bloch snores like a hog.

BUMBOY: *(Snickering.)* Yeah.

FRANZ: They fit you well, Bumboy . . . the clothes. *(Bumboy does not agree.)* I wouldn't lie to you. No man is bonded to another.

BUMBOY: *(Peering at Bloch before speaking.)* Boy.

FRANZ: You're not a boy. You're wearing men's shirts and pants.

BUMBOY: Sock?

FRANZ: *(Grinning.)* And a man's sock.

BUMBOY: *(Pensive.)* Man? No! *(Steadfast.)* BUMBOY!

FRANZ: There's a design to your life, Bumboy. Bloch doesn't give you credit for breathing. *(Pause.)* Don't ever forget the transport.

Bumboy cringes slightly.

FRANZ: Do you remember?

Bumboy looks for help from Bloch, but he is asleep.

FRANZ: He considers you garbage, Bumboy. Listen to your name. Are you a stray?

BUMBOY: *(Sadly.)* Yeah.

FRANZ: You're not a bum. Your family loved you enough to throw you from the cattle cars. You had a family.

BUMBOY: Bloch.

FRANZ: He's not a father. Bloch was going to trade you for a piece of sausage. I've made an offering with the clothes you're wearing. You do like them, don't you?

BUMBOY: Yeah.

FRANZ: They've kept you warm. Those pants will keep you warm when the temperature drops. You'd have had another sock, but Bloch forbade it. He'd rather have you frostbitten than warm.

BUMBOY: *(Knowingly.)* Yeah.

FRANZ: He didn't save your life. Your mother and father did. *(Bumboy is very confused.)* If they catch you, Bloch will be set free and you will be shipped to the resettlement center. They've made certain not to allow anyone to remain alive. *(Pause.)* That's why you're in the forest.

BUMBOY: *(Meekly.)* Bumboy.

FRANZ: You're Bumboy?

BUMBOY: *(Softly.)* Yeah.

FRANZ: You're a transport child, Bumboy. *(Pause.)* I worked at the place where your family was taken. In the resettlement area. They want you back. *(Bumboy lights up with excitement.)* Maybe you won't be able to find them, but they expressed the desire for you to be safe. *(Pause.)* I had an easy enough job there. The families and all the people from the townships would arrive in the cars. Whole sections of the continent, Bumboy. No one was excluded from this gathering.

Ark shifts slightly so that he can listen to Franz more easily.

FRANZ: Can you imagine the screeching brakes of the black locomotives?

BUMBOY: Yeah.

FRANZ: You see, you're not dumb. You're more capable than Bloch cares to admit.

BUMBOY: *(Watching Bloch.)* Not dumb.

ARK: *(Rapidly.)* Did you hear that noise, Franz?

FRANZ: *(Startled.)* Shh! You'll wake him.

ARK: Honest, I heard something.

FRANZ: *(Exasperated.)* Be silent.

ARK: *(Emphatically.)* Bumboy, did you hear it?

Bumboy is not quite sure if he heard anything in the forest.

BUMBOY: Yeah.

ARK: It might be the soldiers with their night maneuvers.

FRANZ: It could be Serbius approaching. Be quiet, now.
ARK: I'll whistle so he can find us.
FRANZ: *(He grabs Ark by the wrist.)* Please, no.
BUMBOY: Plea . . . Please.
FRANZ: Good Bumboy.
ARK: The marshlands are a refuge, Franz. Serbius once told me that humans can survive in them.
FRANZ: Only the young and the healthy. Don't bring it up again.
ARK: The superstitious can't live in there. *(Pause.)* Nor can the old and feeble with bad ears.
FRANZ: *(Concerned about Bloch.)* Let him sleep.
ARK: I'll be quiet until I'm sure of what I hear. *(He returns to his place, but he is still attentive to Franz and Bumboy.)*
FRANZ: You see, Bumboy, you can't remain in the forest.
BUMBOY: No.
FRANZ: They'll come for you. You'll be on one of the endless transports. Transfer stations are being built every day, Bumboy. You're too big now, Bumboy. No one'll throw you out of the next freight car. You'll arrive this time, packed in with other people, where I worked in the resettlement center.
BUMBOY: *(Bewildered.)* Please.
FRANZ: I had a good job. *(Pause.)* The stateless would file out of the cars, and they'd move to the center of the gate. The same special guards that followed you into the forest were pushing the people along. All the luggage and overcoats were checked in at this ticket office. *(Pause.)* It was my job to look through the clothes for jewelry and report it. Often I found cheese and dry crackers in the suitcases. *(Pause.)* Did you ever have cheese as a boy?
BUMBOY: *(Thinking.)* Yeah.
FRANZ: I worked with clothes, Bumboy. I was supposed to heap them back into the cars. Whole tribes of people without any rights came to this transfer point. The ghettos poured them into the cattle cars, Bumboy. *(Bumboy does not understand.)* I came in a transport, too. *(Bumboy is surprised.)* I was young so I worked. I hid one evening in a heap of clothes. The freight car started to roll away and I was in it. I escaped, but I saw what happened to the people. The smokestacks and the piles of clothing. *(Pause.)* I need you, Bumboy, because you would have been there.
ARK: *(Pause.)* I have to go.

FRANZ: Ark?

ARK: In the trees over there. *(Franz nods and Ark exits.)*

FRANZ: You must listen to me, Bumboy.

BUMBOY: Yeah.

FRANZ: *(Firmly.)* The guards'll kill you, Bumboy.

BUMBOY: *(Frightened.)* No.

FRANZ: Like lice. *(Bumboy is perplexed.)* They'll drop you into the smokestacks, Bumboy. All the aberrations of humanity are there, festering in soot. You'll be the chimney sweep. You can record every horror and face you see. A whole continent, Bumboy, is traced on the inside walls of the chimney. You were saved for a reason.

BUMBOY: *(He hesitates. Finally he decides.)* Yeah. *(He points to Bloch.)*

FRANZ: When you learn, you can leave him.

ARK: *(He hurries into the clearing as he pulls up his trousers. Excited.)* Franz, Franz.

FRANZ: You went too far into the forest.

ARK: Franz, the boots! I heard the boots pounding the dirt.

Bumboy becomes alarmed and is about to wake up Bloch.

FRANZ: Bumboy, no. Ark, you're mistaken.

ARK: I swear to you, Franz, not this time. At first I thought it was Serbius, so I moved in a little closer . . . but I heard several voices. It's them, the special guard.

FRANZ: *(Confused.)* So, it comes to this.

BUMBOY: Bloch?

ARK: He'll be safe. It's you, Bumboy . . . and Franz. You must run away. If they catch the two of you . . . you'll be transported.

FRANZ: *(Yielding.)* I'll die in the freight cars.

BUMBOY: *(Pleading.)* No.

ARK: You have a chance. Go into the marshlands. Run straight ahead and don't make any turn, understand?

FRANZ: Yes, Ark, but I can't leave you alone in this clearing.

ARK: I'm a wrinkled old man with punctured eardrums. Let me be. If you take time to glance over your shoulder, you'll run into a tree. And if you make a wrong turn, you'll perish in the forest.

FRANZ: And Bloch?

ARK: He's snoring. Go. Hurry, quickly . . . I'll whistle so that you can have a point of departure.

FRANZ: *(Pause.)* They're sure to locate you.
ARK: Take the boy!
FRANZ: Bumboy!

Bumboy hesitates for a second.

FRANZ: Boy?
BUMBOY: Yeah. *(Bumboy and Franz exit stage center into the remaining forest and the beginning of the marshland.)*
ARK: Bloch, you and I can wait for Serbius. It's so awfully still in that dark forest. *(Pause.)* The last boy has left. Now I can whistle for Serbius. *(He begins to whistle. Initially the whistle is long and pierces the night air.)*
BLOCH: *(A little restless, but still asleep, mumbling.)* Bumboy?
ARK: *(Pause.)* Yeah.
BLOCH: Good Bumboy.

Bloch continues to sleep. The lights begin to fade as Ark whistles for his son.

CURTAIN

Selected Bibliography

This bibliography, intended only to suggest a few studies of possible interest to the reader, includes published works and an occasional manuscript which make reference to Cuban-born playwrights presently living in the United States. The bibliography also includes other Cuban-born playwrights, dead or living elsewhere, whose works have been staged in this country and are becoming part of a tradition within the theatrical movement of Cuban expatriates.

Alba-Buffill, Elio. "Los perros jíbaros: dolor de Cuba hecho arte." *Tribu* (1983): 17-19.

Benedetti, Mario. "Situación actual de la cultura cubana." In: Benedetti, Mario. *Literatura y arte nuevo en Cuba.* Barcelona: Editorial Estela, 1971.

Colecchia, Francesca. "Matías Montes Huidobro: His Theater." *Latin American Theater Review* (Summer, 1980): 77-80.

Cruz-Luis, Adolfo. "El movimiento teatral cubano en la revolución." *Casa de las Américas* 113 (1979): 40-50.

De Paula, Paulo. "Theater in Exile. The Cuban Theater in Miami." A Master of Arts Thesis. Northeast Missouri State University, 1987.

"Entrevista a dos dramaturgos cubanos." *Dramaturgos* 1, 2 (July-August, 1987): 4-5. (Interviews with Raúl de Cárdenas and José Corrales).

Escarpanter, José A. "Entrevista a tres voces." *Guángara Libertaria* 8, 29 (Winter, 1987): 12-15. (With Leopoldo Hernández).

______ . "Veinticinco años de teatro cubano en el exilio." *Latin American Theater Review* (Spring, 1986): 57-66.

Estrada, Hall. "Three by Three: Un logro." *Dramaturgos* 1, 1 (May-June, 1987): 7.

Febles, Jorge. "La desfiguración enajenante en *Ojos para no ver*." *Cuadernos Hispanoamericanos* 4, 2 (1982): 127-136.

Fernández Vázquez, Antonio A. "Lo sagrado y lo profano en *La rebelión de los negros.*" In: Martín, Gregorio C., editor, *Selected Proceedings: Thirty-second Mountain Interstate Foreign Language Conference.* Winston Salem, NC: Wake Forest University, 1984, 131-136.

González-Cruz, Luis F. "The Art of Julio Matas." *Latin American Literary Review* 1, 1 (Fall, 1972): 125-128.

______ . "Virgilio Piñera y el teatro del absurdo en Cuba." *Mester* 5, 1 (November, 1974): 52-58.

González-Cruz, Luis F. "Matías Montes Huidobro." *Latin American Literary Review* 2, 4 (Spring-Summer, 1974): 163-170.

______ . "Arte y situación de Virgilio Piñera." *Caribe* 2, 2 (Fall, 1977): 77-86.

______ . "El teatro de Julio Matas." *Linden Lane Magazine* 4, 4 (October-December, 1985): 24-25.

______ . *Virgilio Piñera. "Una caja de zapatos vacía."* A Critical Edition. Miami: Universal, 1986.

______ . "En torno a *Una caja de zapatos vacía* de Virgilio Piñera." *El Miami Herald*, May 8, 1987: 8.

______ . "Virgilio Piñera se estrena en Miami." *Dramaturgos* 1, 1 (May-June, 1987): 2.

______ . "Virgilio Piñera, anticomunista. *Los siervos*, una obra olvidada." *El Miami Herald*, June 19, 1987: 9-10.

______ . "El misterio de Electra Garrigó." *El Miami Herald*, October 1, 1987: 6.

______ . "Julio Matas." In: Kanellos, Nicolás, editor. *Biographical Dictionary of Hispanic Literature in the United States.* Westport, CT: Greenwood Press, 1989, 187-192.

______ . "Julio Matas." In: Martínez, Julio A., editor. *Dictionary of Twentieth-Century Cuban Literature*. Westport, CT: Greenwood Press, 1990, 292-296.

______ . "Virgilio Piñera." In: Martínez, Julio A., editor. *Dictionary of Twentieth-Century Cuban Literature.* Westport, CT: Greenwood Press, 1990, 361-370.

González Freire, Natividad. *Teatro cubano 1927-1961*. Havana: Ministerio de Relaciones Exteriores, 1961.

González Reigosa, Fernando. "Las culturas del exilio." *Boletín del Instituto de Estudios Cubanos* [Madrid] (October, 1976).

Hospital, Carolina. "*Las provisiones* y el teatro popular en Cuba." *Linden Lane Magazine* 5, 4 (October-December, 1986): 10-11.

Jackson, May H. "*Comedy of the Dead* by José Cid Pérez." In: Gutiérrez de la Solana, Alberto and Elio Alba-Buffill, editors. *José Cid Pérez*. New York: Senda Nueva de Ediciones, 1981, 51-56.

Jiménez, Onilda A. "Simposium sobre teatro." *Noticias de arte* 7, 6 (June, 1982): 12.

Leal, Rine. "Algunas consideraciones sobre el teatro cubano." *Insula* 260-261 (July-August, 1968): 4-5.

______ . *Breve historia del teatro cubano.* Havana: Editorial Letras Cubanas, 1980.

______ . *En primera persona. 1954-1966*. Havana: Instituto del Libro, 1967 (Contemporary theater criticism).

Leiva, Roberto. "Nuestro teatro en dos décadas de exilio." *Diario Las Américas*, January 6, 1979: sec. B, p. 11.

Martí de Cid, Dolores. "El ser y el hacer en el teatro de José Cid Pérez." *Folio* (December, 1984): 89-106.

Matas, Julio. "Theater and Cinematography." In: Mesa-Lago, Carmelo, editor. *Revolutionary Change in Cuba.* Pittsburgh: University of Pittsburgh Press, 1971, pp. 427-445.

______ . "Teatro cubano del exilio." *Dramaturgos* 1, 1 (May-June, 1987): 8.

Montes Huidobro, Matías. *Persona, vida y máscara en el teatro cubano.* Miami: Universal, 1973.

______ . "Teatro en *Lunes de Revolución.*" *Latin American Theater Review* (Fall, 1984): 17-34.

______ . "Continuidad teatral." *Dramaturgos* 1, 1 (May-June, 1987): 3-6.

Muguercia, Magaly. "El 'Teatro de arte' en Cuba entre 1936 y 1950." *Tablas* [Havana] 4 (1984): 2-15.

"La obra que esperó veinte años." An interview with Luis F. González-Cruz. *El Miami Herald*, May 1, 1987: 9.

Palls, Terry L. "El carácter del teatro cubano contemporáneo." *Latin American Theater Review* 13 (Summer, 1980): 51-58.

Pogolotti, Graziella, Rine Leal, Rosa Ileana Boudet. *Teatro y revolución.* Havana: Editorial Letras Cubanas, 1980.

Rodríguez Sardiñas, Orlando. "Texto del teatro cubano contemporáneo en el contexto revolucionario." In: Gutiérrez de la Solana, Alberto and Elio Alba-Buffill, editors. *José Cid Pérez.* New York: Senda Nueva de Ediciones, 1981, 125-137.

Sánchez-Boudy, José. *Historia de la literatura cubana en el exilio.* Miami: Universal, 1975.

Watson-Espener, Maida. "Ethnicity and the Hispanic American Stage: The Cuban Experience." In: Kanellos, Nicolás. *Two Hundred Years of Hispanic Theater.* Houston: Arte Público Press, 1985, 34-44.

______ . "Teatro y mujeres." In: *Hispanos en los Estados Unidos.* Madrid: Universidad Complutense (Instituto de Cooperación Iberoamericana), 1987.

______ . "Themes and Techniques in Contemporary Cuban Exile Theater." In: *A Thematic Analysis and Sourcebook for Hispanic Literature in the United States.* Westport, CT: Greenwood Press, in press.

Woodyard, George. "Perspectives in Cuban Theater." *Revista/Review Interamericana* 9 (1979): 41-49.